FRAGMENTS OF A JOURNAL

Fragments
of a Journal

by EUGÈNE IONESCO

translated by Jean Stewart

Grove Press, Inc., New York

Scattered Images of Childhood

I have never been to Beauchamps. There's no road to take you there. It's a tiny village, lost in the meadows, a few kilometres from La Chapelle-Anthenaise. You reach it along old tracks. 'It's over that way,' Marie tells me, pointing. 'But now it's autumn, the way's muddy, we shan't be able to go there till the spring.'

*

From the top of the hill I can see the Mill, its old roof hidden in the mist.

*

It's prize-giving day. We are all sitting on our benches, without textbooks or exercise-books or satchels, in our Sunday best. Beside the teacher's desk there's a whole pile of books, bound in red or blue. Monsieur Guéné takes about ten of them and hands them out to the first-form pupils. Then he fetches another dozen and hands them out to us. My book is red. I open it: geographical descriptions, hunting stories. I am disappointed. I'd rather have had a nice story-book.

*

My mother comes to fetch me. It's autumn. 'You've got to come back to Paris,' she tells me. 'We aren't living in the hotel now. We've got a small flat where we're going to live with your granny and grandfather in the rue de l'Avre. It's quite close to Aunt Sabine's. You can't stay on here, you've got to be educated.' 'I can stay on here,' I told her. 'M. Guéné has promised me I'd pass my certificate this year at Laval.' 'That's not the same thing,' she answered, 'that's not the same thing.' I remember those tall Paris houses. How can I bear to leave the fields? 'You know,' she tells me, 'Paris has changed. The war's been over for a long time, it's quite different, quite different. There are fêtes going on all the time, it's lots of fun: roundabouts, shows, lights, lots of lights. It's all lit up at night. And Aunt Sabine has a fine drawing-room. She entertains fashionable people. She gives parties.'

We go to see old Guéné so that I can say goodbye to him.... I can't quite remember where: in his office at the Mairie? No, on the floor above, I believe, in his own home. There's somebody else too, a woman in a black dress. Not his wife, for he wasn't married. His maid? Did he have a maid? It must have been the charwoman for the Mairie and the school. Monseiur Guéné stands there. 'It's a pity,' he says, 'he'd have gone up into the first form, he'd have got his certificate this year. I'm going to kiss you.' He bends down to kiss me and I feel his big moustache.

*

It's time to go. I'm feeling more cheerful. I'm looking forward to the fêtes in Paris. Paris never used to be like that. I imagine merry-go-rounds, all lit up, gorgeous illuminations, ladies in fine dresses, people singing in the streets, fireworks, a sumptuous drawing-room.

Père Baptiste is there in his blue smock, with his whip round his neck. The mare is harnessed to the trap. I hug Maurice, who is to stay on at the Mill by himself all winter. I hug Mère Jeannette, who's on the verge of tears. She hurries back into the house: 'It's just like little Armand,' she says. We make our way to the station, in the rain. We climb out. Père Baptiste kisses me, wipes away a tear with the stump of his thumb and then quickly turns away.

I never saw Mère Jeannette or Père Baptiste again.

*

At gym time, before we got our drill-instructor, our only form of physical training was to walk round and round the school yard, singing. I would yell, with all the strength in my lungs: 'Long live our flag, the glorious flag of France.' 'Not so loud, Ionesco,' Monsieur Guéné would interrupt me in full swing, 'not so loud, you're singing out of tune. Let the others sing, they do it better.'

*

When the bells toll for a funeral I am overcome with a mysterious anguish, a sort of fascination. We know all the people who die.

*

Children get bored. I used to get bored in Paris. At the Mill I am never bored, even when it rains, except perhaps when I have nothing to read.

*

8

I'm in love with Ribot's little sister. Yet Beauplet's little sister is much prettier.

*

Père Baptiste had never been to Paris. He had once been to Le Mans, when he was young, to enlist. It was by firing his pistol to celebrate his enlistment that he had blown off his thumb. 'I had my handkerchief round it,' he said, 'I didn't do it on purpose.' And so the military tribunal had acquitted him. But nobody was quite sure that he had not done it on purpose. He could neither read nor write. To count, he used to make little notches with a penknife in a piece of wood (he must have had a complicated system: tiny notches for the ones, bigger notches for the tens and hundreds, different shapes for the thousands).

*

There were some American soldiers billeted on the peasants in the village, waiting to go back to America; a hundred and fifty or two hundred of them. On Sundays they put on their broad-brimmed hats like those Boy Scouts wear today. They belonged to a medical corps. They stopped a whole winter; most distracting for the village people! From time to time an officer came from Argentré to inspect them. At La Chapelle-Anthenaise there was only a sergeant-major, a very red-faced man who was said to be bad-tempered. He had huge stripes on his sleeves. In the evening he held roll-call in the Church square. The rest of the time he left them alone. Where did the sergeant-major live? I believe it was at Père Grudé's, the former mayor, who was grocer, saddle-maker, innkeeper in a small way; he had a couple of rooms for travellers, which were always empty. At the Mill there was an American living in the room upstairs, the middle one: a small fair man, a dancing-master. He used to bring his friends along; there was one who was a singer and who was billeted at Argentré. They would gather round the fireside, four or five of them. Mère Jeannette loved listening to the singer, who accompanied himself on a guitar or a mandolin. After some time, though, she'd had enough of it. One day when it had rained a great deal, the water had risen, the stream had turned into a muddy river. The courtyard was flooded. The water came right up to the door of the farm. "Well, at least it'll keep them away," said Mère Jeannette. It didn't keep them away,

9

though, for they had discovered the back door. One of them, who was a cook or a pastrycook, made us a delicious cake with a chocolate cream filling. We all had a real feast—the children, Mère Jeannette, Marie and Père Baptiste and the Americans. Père Baptiste was very fond of them. The dancer spoke French badly, the singer better; he had lived in Paris. Mère Jeannette was amazed to hear him speak French. 'It's because he lived in Paris before the war,' Marie said. 'All the same,' Mère Jeannette replied, 'he *is* an American.' In the evening, before roll-call, they had their dinner. They had set up their kitchens in the village, and after they had been served they distributed what was left among the inhabitants. Out of tact, they never gave away meat dishes: only sweets, cakes or chocolate custard. I was sent to bring back some of this in a pan. An American soldier dipped a ladle into the pot and poured out custard into my pan. One evening they all packed into big army lorries and drove off. The village seemed very empty afterwards. The dancing master sent a postcard or two, and wrote a letter to Simone to tell her to come to America when she grew up and learn dancing there.

*

When did I first notice that time 'passed'? The sense of time was not at first associated with the idea of death. Of course, when I was four or five years old I realized that I should grow older and older and that I should die. At about seven or eight, I said to myself that my mother would die some day and the thought terrified me. I knew she would die before me. However, I thought of it as a decisive interruption of the present, for everything was in the present. A day, an hour, seemed to me long, limitless; I could see no end to it. When they talked to me about next year I had the feeling that next year would never come. When I was at La Chapelle-Anthenaise I felt outside of time, in a sort of Paradise. At about eleven or twelve, not before, I first became intuitively aware that things would end. I used to go with grandfather and grandmother, my mother and Aunt Sabine to a little cinema in the avenue de Suffren. It was a source of great wonderment to me. We looked forward to this treat; I looked forward to it. When we all set forth, pushing my grandmother, who was an invalid, in a wheelchair, and made our way from the rue de l'Avre to the avenue de Suffren, my joy was clouded by the thought that our pleasure would not last, that the film would come to an end and that eventually we should go home. It would go on for a long, a very long time, two or three hours, but that long time had its limits. Expectation made me aware of time: I could not be happy without something to look forward to, some particular joy, holidays, Christmas, Thursdays, a visit to some friends of my mother's outside the city on a Sunday; but when I was eight or nine, when I lived at the Mill, everything was joy, everything was presentness. The seasons seemed to spread out in space. The world was a decorative background, with its colours, now dark and now bright, with its flowers and grass appearing, then disappearing, coming towards us, moving away from us, unfolding before our eyes while we ourselves stayed in the same place, watching time pass, ourselves being outside time. Because of that, no doubt, anyone's death seemed mysterious, illogical, terrible: an emptiness in the present. Then, all of a sudden, there came a kind of reversal; it was as though a centrifugal force had projected me out of my immutability into the midst of the things that go and come back and go away for good. Worse still, I suddenly had the feeling that things stood still, while I was moving away from them. At fifteen or sixteen it was all over, I was in time, in flight, in finiteness. The present had disappeared, there was nothing left for me but a past and a tomorrow, a tomorrow which I was already conscious of as past.

Since then I have tried, every day, to cling on to something stable, I have tried desperately to recover a present, to establish it, to widen it. I have travelled in search of an intact world over which time would have no power. Indeed, two days' travel, the discovery of an unfamiliar city slow down the rush of events. Two days in a new country are worth thirty spent in the place we are used to, days shortened by triteness, debased by familiarity. Familiarity smooths down time, so that you slip on it as on an over-polished floor. A world that is new, a world that is for ever new, a world that is for ever, young for ever, that is Paradise. Speed is not only infernal, it is hell itself, it is the Fall, accelerated. The present has been, Time has been, neither present nor Time exist any longer, the geometrical progression of our fall has flung us into nothingness.

*

I was five years old, I think; a children's home, not far from Paris, run by the local authorities. Where was it? Somewhere near Longjumeau? To get there you went by train from a station underground: was it the Invalides or the Gare du Luxembourg, for the Sceaux line? I stayed several months in this home. Separated from my mother, I was unhappy all the time, I never got used to separation, nor to the communal dormitory and refectory, nor to the all-pervading, intolerable presence of other people. It was not that I wasn't fond of them, I had friends, a great many friends, but I never had play-fellows. At five, I was already an individualist. My mother came to visit me once a fortnight: she would appear and disappear, not in time, but in a kind of immense space. When she left again on Sunday night, it was for ever, a fortnight was for ever. An emptiness in the present. I remember the place vaguely, or rather, quite well: the dormitory, the high walls and railings round the park in which we lived and which was just a prison yard to me. Communal meals: the tin spoons and forks and plates, the pewter mugs, and that smell of disinfectant in the lavatories and white-washed passages. (At the age of twenty, when I did my military service, I encountered it all again: dormitories, white-washed walls, a vast prison yard and the horrible smell of disinfectant. I was as wretched then as at five years old; I became a five-year-old child again.) I remember one 'big boy', he must have been about twelve, who had tried to climb over the railings and had hurt his testicles and been carried to the infirmary, bleeding; I remember one of my small companions who fell ill and was also taken to the infirmary, and died there; I remember a heart-rending scene: I clung howling to my mother to keep her from going, and the matron had difficulty in persuading her not to take me with her. I remember another Sunday when my mother and I were picking up chestnuts in the grass in a part of the park where we were only allowed to go with our parents, when they came to visit us. I remember, too, seeing my first play there, in a hall with benches. Some peasants in blue smocks were on the stage, playing cards. One of them got angry, got up and said something or other, I don't remember. Who were these suburban players? The angry peasant was an old man.

*

The big boys played cards in our dormitory. They were allowed to. I stole their pack of cards. I don't remember where I hid it. They complained to the matron, suspecting everyone but me. And after I had taken advantage of the dormitory being empty to put the cards back on the table, how amazed they were to find them there.

*

Once my mother came with my young aunt and uncle. They took me outside, beyond the iron railings, to the nearby inn; we drank lemonade, and they danced to the sound of a pianola. Then we went for a walk in the little village; just a couple of hundred yards, but what a treat, how wonderful the world was beyond the gates!

*

I have just recalled that village in the light of a summer Sunday. It is still a blessed place, as it used to be; a tiny village; but I am no longer there. Who are these boys in their Sunday best?

*

1963: Robert has now left the Mill. He had leased it from Marie, who has sold the farm to a big landowner, unfairly, for Robert had a right of pre-emption since he was working the land. They went to law about it. A caretaker is living in the house. It's Sunday, he's not there, he is at Mass. Through the open window we look into the big room. It is empty. Only the old clock is still there, in its corner; the bin and the table have gone. They have blocked up the hearth and put in electricity. The garden has been neglected; it is overgrown with tall weeds and nettles. It's a wilderness. Wild flowers. The currant bush is still there. Opposite, the hedges round Père Dalibard's field, sloping up towards La Brochardière. The place where the Mill stands is still as soft and gentle as ever, like a natural nest. The bridge over the pond is broken. How do they manage to cross, in winter, when it becomes a stream again?

Nowadays Marie lives in a comfortable house in Saint-Jean. She is seventy-six, and seems to have grown younger. She still has the same streak of hardness, combined with excessive emotionalism. A gift of money sets her weeping. And yet she is really very fond of us. Her eyes fill with tears when she sees us. Simone often goes to see her. Maurice hasn't gone for years. He has bought a house in the village. Raymond has broken with her too. I should have liked to have the Mill house. The old slate roofs are in good condition, the walls still solid. I have never asked her for her Mill house. 'I'd have liked to keep it for you,' she tells me. She says the same to Simone. She used to say it to Raymond. Maurice and Raymond wanted to buy it from her and to pay her a life annuity as well. She would not consent. That was why they quarrelled. Simone and I have lunch with Marie. Simone has bought and prepared the chicken; she has bought bread, wine and sausage. Maurice has killed a rabbit. I ask Marie if any of Père Baptiste's tipple is left. She sets the bottle of Calvados on the table, but brings no glasses.

★

There were 680 inhabitants in the village when I was a small boy. In 1939 there were 450. Two years ago, when Marie left the Mill to go to Saint-Jean, there were only 300. Now things are improving. Peasants who no longer cultivate their own land but get jobs at Laval as railwaymen, roundsmen, bricklayers or labourers have come back to their houses at La Chapelle-Anthenaise. They all have cars. They can get to Laval in ten minutes in their small cars, whereas formerly it meant an hour's drive in the trap or else you had to take the train. Nowadays they like living in the country; they go to Laval to work and come back in the evening.

★

What mischief had I been up to? I tell Marie I'm sorry, she kisses me and comforts me: 'You're a good little boy all the same.'

★

The elder that used to grow near the paddock has been gone a long time. Poor old elder. We used to cut off the small branches to make into cigarettes. We went to smoke them under the apple-tree with the big red apples, in the middle of the meadow. With the two *sous* I had given Raymond to pay the rent of the 'hut' he had lent me, he bought a real little cigar and smoked it all alone, in front of us.

*

I am ill in bed in the little room. Is it flu, perhaps, or a quinsy? A cow is sick, too, in the stable. The vet has been sent for. After he has seen to the cow, Père Baptiste brings him up into my room. The vet is very tall and thin, about forty-five to fifty years old, with a little brown moustache. He says it's nothing serious, after looking at my throat and taking my pulse. He tells Marie what to do for me, then they offer him a drink.

*

We never managed to catch more than five or six minnows when we went fishing. Except once, when I caught thirty or forty of them. Marie fried them, and I was very proud. When the water was clear we used to lie flat on our stomachs at the edge of the stream, without moving, and we could see the fish. Once, in a dark corner, under a root growing in the water, I caught sight of a bigger fish, that kept quite still, watching the others probably. Was it a gudgeon?

*

A long, long walk along the old lanes with Uncle Alexandre, who has come from Paris to see me. A clearing, a farm at the edge of a field: a plum tree. We steal some plums, we fill our pockets with them—mine and Alexandre's. Then we go to the farm. What did Alexandre want to buy from the farmer's wife? Milk, and butter? Marie had plenty of those, and masses of eggs; rillettes, too. Perhaps some Calvados. 'You needn't have hidden to pick up my plums, I saw you, you could have asked me for them. I give them away.' At the Mill, I take the plums out of my pockets. My clothes are all stained.

*

All this has gradually withered away. It became as thin as a leaf, as thin and transparent as a sliver of glass; transparent, then it broke noiselessly and disappeared.

15

First of all there was a slight deterioration, barely perceptible: a spoonful scooped out of a bath of honey. It spread and deepened. After a time, when nobody was thinking about it, a cry was heard that might be described as shrill. It may have been the barley growing, or the shoots shooting, or the chutes chuting, or some tool boring into whatever was there. We never knew. We did not notice: it was the war, all those preoccupations of ours, those preoccupations of hours, the Occupation and other barbarisms. Very Turkish. Then there was navigation, mountaineering, roamings and ramblings. 'Our debauchery was wonderful, Madeleine!' Ah, life is meant to be lived: I had this precept from my grandfather, the preceptor's preceptor. One night, at nightfall, seven o'clock at night maybe, those fortunate people who had mirrors would see the tiny hole, tiny but growing, made in the immense blackness, though immense is a euphemism, it must have been limitless perhaps. I always have to say 'perhaps' because of the uncertainty and inadequacy of the evidence.

One fine morning, at three o'clock in the afternoon, the people of all nations thought they noticed that something was going wrong, or was going off. Some of them summoned their mothers, others called the Mayor, others their supervisor, and those that lived in the avenue du Maine summoned the Chairman of the Parish Council. These eminent figures assured them with a smile that the thing was an accomplished fact: don't pay any attention, enjoy yourselves, have a good time, debauchery is at your disposal, Madeleine, isn't life meant to be lived? don't you fancy the preceptor's precept? Come now, don't worry, don't be so childish! Come now, come now, come now, show some sense.

Come now, come now, come now, they repeated in chorus, the people, the parishioners. All obeyed this order and went off for the week-end; they made no other plans, they showed no more surprise. The Establishment had spoken.

I, for my part, being allergic to injunctions, wanted to think it over…
alas, it was lost labour. I did what the rest did. What decision could I take, having no mirrors of my own, nor yet being one of the mob? I am a proud man, of another era.

Participation, identification: Brecht wants no magical, emotional participation in the theatre, he does not want us, or says he does not want us to identify ourselves with his characters, he wants us to understand them, he seeks this understanding. In fact, it is his thought, his ideology that becomes the magical element. He wants us to participate in, to identify ourselves with his thought, I mean his faith or what he takes for faith. All committed writers seek to violate you, to convince you, to enlist you.

When one of them shows me, on the stage, police firing on exploited workers, he does it so that I may become, by magic, the worker, so that I may share in his pain, stand by his side, identify myself with him.

Not so long ago, there were plays that showed how the Jews corrupted civilization by their subversive, demoralizing ideas, by money, etc., etc., trying to make the spectator identify himself with the Nazi character who killed the Jews.

But nowadays, since it's become quite easy, since nobody objects, since at one time it was forbidden to oppose Fascism and now it's allowed and approved of, I see plays that show how the Nazis massacred Jewish women and children and old men, I am moved to indignation and of course I want revenge, I become the Jew.

(They never show us how the Algerians put out the eyes of French children, that's not done; they don't show us on the stage how the Chinese massacred the Tibetans, that's not done either.)

So, too, to take a slighter example: we identify ourselves with the wife of a tyrannical husband, when he is shown as a tyrant; we identify ourselves with the husband when we are shown how vicious the wife is.

Any author who is described as objective, or fair, or sensible, or realistic, has a bad character to be punished and a good one to be rewarded. That's why any realistic or committed play is mere melodrama.

But if, instead of talking about the wicked German, or Japanese, or Russian, or French, or American soldier, or the wicked bourgeois, or the criminal incendiary, or the horrible militarist, or the treacherous deserter, etc., if instead of all that I strip man of the inhumanity belonging to his class, his race, his bourgeois—or other—status: when I look behind all this, and speak of what is an intimate part of myself, of my fear, my longings, my anguish, my delight in being; or when I give free reign to my unfettered imagination, to my imaginative constructions, I am not only being myself, I am not being a partisan, I am not taking sides with one against another, I am no longer myself alone but I am all the others in their essential humanity, I am not the good man or the bad man, or a bourgeois, I no longer belong to any class or race or to this army or to that army.

But I am man, stripped of any sort of partisan mentality, of segregation, of dehumanisation, of alienation by choice or party loyalty, and I no longer hate others. This is the sphere of profound identification, this is the way to attain it.

Jules Verne, the last visionary writer. What he imagined has become reality.

Two possible attitudes:
To imagine, because imagining means foreseeing. What we imagine is now true, what we imagine will be realized. Science fiction is becoming, or has already become, realistic literature.
A second possible attitude: to consider reality as something beyond reality, to be aware of it not as surrealistic but as unfamiliar miraculous, a-real. Reality of the unreal, unreality of the real.

I was born quite a long time ago.
A very long time, and yet a very short time ago. I haven't yet succeeded in understanding what has happened to me. I have very little time left to understand what I have not yet understood, and I scarcely think I shall manage to do so. I have not managed to accept existence and to accept myself. I can see nothing beyond the beings and things that surround me and that seem to me enigmas, more or less. I can never, or seldom, or with great difficulty, get on with other people, because I cannot get on with myself

either. The forms of satisfaction I have sought, and found, to fill my life, its emptiness, its nostalgia, have sometimes succeeded, but how inadequately, in disguising the malaise of existence. They once distracted me, but can no longer do so. Pain, grief, failure have always seemed to me truer than success or pleasure. I have always tried to live, but I have passed life by. I think that is what most men feel. To forget oneself one must not only forget one's own death, but forget that those one loves will die and that the world will come to an end. The thought of the end fills me with anguish and fury. I have never been really happy except when drunk. Unfortunately alcohol destroys memory and I have only retained blurred recollections of my moments of euphoria. Life is unhappiness. That does not prevent me from preferring life to death, existence to non-existence, because I am not sure of being once I have ceased to exist. Existence being the only mode of being I know, I cling to this existence, for I cannot, alas, imagine any mode of being apart from existence.

I am limited and alienated, others are limited and alienated, and all forms of action, of revolution, of literature are only ways of forgetting alienation for a moment, not remedies for alienation. The end of it all can only be an even more lucid, hence more desperate, awakening.

I cannot help laughing bitterly when I see all around me believing they believe, and being engulfed.

A vast weariness overwhelms me: presumably psychological in origin, with no apparent cause, but the cause of which I know: the certain, or almost certain, knowledge that all is vanity.

I have written a whole set of plays, a lot of books to show what everybody knows and to confirm to myself what I have always known: the strangeness of the universe, the banality of ordinary life shot through by horror, etc. This implies that I became adult very young. Not on every plane.

Why, I wonder, have I taken so much trouble if my own writing, that's to say my enquiry into what is called the self and what is called reality, has not taken me one step further towards knowledge, illumination or serenity?

All that I know now, I have known since the age of six or seven, the 'age of reason'.

The books I have read, literature or philosophy, but chiefly literature, for I have a concrete rather than an abstract turn of mind and little aptitude for science, the books, the words of others, monuments and works of art and political involvement have never done more than reinforce and underline what I have known almost all my life: the only thing one can know is that death is there waiting for my mother, my family, myself. (I realize now that I never thought my father would die. I was terrified at the thought that my mother was going to die, this was a permanent and agonizing obsession, but the idea of my father's death never entered my head. Was it because I seldom saw him, or because I did not love him? Certainly not, for I did love him and his long absence created in me, in all of us, a sense of emptiness, an immense longing, a wound. I did not think about his death because he seemed to me, perhaps, so strong as to be immortal.)

There is a golden age: the age of childhood, of ignorance; as soon as one knows one is going to die, childhood is over. As I said, it ended very soon for me. So one can be grown up at seven. Then, I believe most human beings forget what they have understood, recover another sort of childhood that, for some of them, for a very few, can last all their lives. It is not a true childhood but a kind of forgetting. Desires and anxieties are there, preventing you from having access to the essential truth.

I never lapsed into forgetfulness, I never recovered childhood. Apart from childhood and forgetfulness there is only grace that can console one for existing or give one plenitude, heaven on earth and in one's heart. Children, in their restlessness, are unaware of grace. There is no other state but this. How can we go on living without grace? And yet we do go on living.

If I tell these private thoughts of mine, it is because I know they are not mine alone, and that practically everyone is trying to say the same things and that the writer is only a man who says out loud what other people think or whisper. Even if I thought that what I am confessing is not a universal confession but the expression of an individual experience, I should confess it all the same in the hope of being cured or of finding relief. But I have no such hope, we have no such hope; we share a common distress. Then, why? What good can it do? It's because, in spite of everything, we cannot but become aware, become more acutely aware of a certain reality, the reality of the unhappiness of existing, the fact that the human condition is beyond bearing: a useless awareness, which cannot but be, and which finds expression, such is literature.

Ever since I was fifteen, that's to say from that moment when I lost all that was left me of my childhood, from the moment when I ceased to be aware of the present and knew only the past hurrying into the future, that's to say into the abyss, ever since I became fully conscious of time I have felt old and I have wanted to live. I have run after life as though to catch time, and I've tried to live. I have run after life so much that it has always escaped me, I have run, I have never been late and never too early, and yet I have never caught up with it: it's as though I had run alongside of it.

What is life? I may be asked. For me, life is not Time; it is not this state of existence, for ever escaping us, slipping between our fingers and vanishing like a ghost as soon as you try to grasp it. For me it is, it must be, the present, presentness, plenitude. I have run after life so much that I have lost it.

I am at the age when you grow ten years older in one year, when an hour is only a few minutes long and you cannot even note the passing quarters. And yet I still run after life in the hope of catching it at the last minute, as one jumps on to the steps of the last carriage of a moving train.

I remember the quarter of an hour break at my primary school. A quarter of an hour! what a long, busy space of time; enough to think of one game, play it, end it, start another. . . .

Of course, even before I was fifteen, I had had this sense of time passing. Thursdays and Sundays went by; I mean that I knew they were going by. Discovering time means being aware of its passage, believing and indeed being sure that tomorrow will come, waiting for something, expecting something.

I had always been told that the days followed one another, that the seasons came to an end. Of course, this was what they told me and I was bound to believe what grown-up people and the schoolmaster asserted. I had been told it, granted. But 'next year' was only a word; and even if I believed that this 'next year' would one day come, it seemed so far away that it wasn't worth thinking about; the time in between was as long as eternity; so it was just as if it was never going to come. You made no plans, you could make none, since it was so far ahead, so very far ahead. ... In any case, though tomorrow was going to come, though the seasons would end and then return, it was they that would go and come back, while I should stay in the same place. The sun and the stars moved around me, who stood still at the centre of everything. The earth and its colours and its fields and its snow and rain all moved around me. I don't know at what point it was that I must have taken a sort of step. How did it happen? From that moment onward I became aware of the past. I ought not to have stirred, I was swept into the dance, caught up in the whirling movement of things. Being in Time means running after the present. You run after things, you run with things, you flow away.

At seven years old I was in Paris. At eight, in the country. I wonder if while I was living in the country I still thought of death. Of course I wanted to see my mother, who was working in Paris to pay for my keep. But when I was away from my mother I was happier, all the same. It was when I was with her that I thought about death, about her death, about my own. When I was alone, I mean without her, though with other people and children, I no longer experienced this anguish, I never or hardly ever felt it. As a matter of fact I don't believe the idea of death was connected with the idea of time. For the people who died were just people who had 'left us', who had not waited for their death but had gone away. Going away means space, not time. And yet this is not quite true. For when I learnt what death is I learnt, too, that my mother would die some day and that we should surely, ineluctably, come to that day. So it must have been the thought that my mother would die, not today but one day, a fixed day, that gave me the idea of time.

I dream that I am told: 'The revelation, the answer to all your questions can only come to you in a dream. You must have a dream.' So, in my dream, I fall asleep and I dream, in my dream, that I'm having the absolute dream. On waking, that's to say on really waking, I remember having dreamed that I'd dreamed, but I can remember nothing about the dream within a dream, the dream of absolute truth, the dream that explained everything.

It was a rather complicated business: hillsides, little gardens, a great deal of soft dark earth, autumn, grey skies. Low houses. What else was there? A white cat ran out of the walled kitchen garden where there was no grass, no vegetables, everything was newly sown or already gathered, how could one tell? All at once the cat turned into a girl who said to us (we were suddenly sitting at a long rustic table inside a farm, and there was a little window on my left), 'I've got to get away from my family, I need freedom, I must develop my personality.' This was probably why the white cat had escaped through the little door out of the kitchen garden. She ran and I tried to catch her. 'I want to know what I ought to do, too,' I said. Then scraps: a peasant with a moustache, wearing a cap; then I became the peasant (to whom I had just been talking); apples (where did they come from?) had they fallen from that apple-tree (if it was an apple-tree?) under which people (including myself?) were talking about money; a little meadow, with a hedge round it; an orchard; but why not spring and sunshine? Always that grey lowering autumn sky.

The peasant turns into someone else and counts his money. I look at him. Once again I turn into someone like him, a peasant with a cap and a moustache, as if I were his reflection or he were my reflection in a glass.

After a great many incidents (what were they?) I am exhorted to dream the absolute Dream.

How did all this come about?

I've been telling myself for a considerable time that I ought to begin my real work; for after all, the theatre is not my true vocation. Having written a play, after writing various other things, I wanted to write a second, then having succeeded in interesting some people in this second play I began to write a third. Subsequently, as I managed to make a living by it after the fourth or fifth play, of course I went on writing others and did nothing else. That was how I became a 'playwright', a 'professional man of the theatre'.

I ought to have gone on writing for the theatre and at the same time writing (oh, how I hate that verb 'to write', especially when it's used without a direct object) other things. I should have had more books to my credit, I should have used, improved, invented other systems of expression, I should have constructed other edifices; there would have been, perhaps not other worlds but other creations, more varied aspects and a greater richness within the same creation. As soon as I shake off despair I feel the urge, the overwhelming desire to create.

I could have done so many things, I could have realized so many dreams if weariness, an inconceivable, enormous weariness had not overpowered me for the last fifteen years or so, or even far longer. A weariness that kept me from working but also from resting, from enjoying life and being happy and relaxing, and that also kept me from turning more towards others, as I'd have wished to, instead of being the prisoner of myself, of my weariness, of that weight, that burden which is the burden of my self; how can you turn outwards towards others when your own self weighs you down? No doctor, and I've consulted thirty or forty of them, no doctor has known how to, or been able to, cure this infinite weariness because, presumably, not one of them has gone to the source, the deep-seated cause of my trouble. I myself am increasingly aware of the reason for my exhaustion: it is that perennial doubt, the sense of 'What's the use?' that seems to have been rooted in my mind all my life and that I cannot get rid of. Oh, if that 'What's the use?' had not germinated in my soul, then shot up, then spread over everything, choking all other plants, I'd have been another man, as another man might say. This is the weed that has absorbed all the water meant for other, more profitable plants, which has prevented them from blooming and has bloomed in their stead.

A finite universe is unimaginable, inconceivable. An infinite universe is unimaginable, inconceivable. Doubtless the universe is neither finite nor infinite, since the finite and the infinite are only man's ways of thinking about it; in any case, that finiteness and infiniteness should only be ways of thinking and speaking is also something inconceivable, unimaginable. We cannot take a single step beyond our own impotence; outside those walls I feel sick and giddy. If the wall is no longer there, the gulf opens at my feet and I am seized with dizziness.

I wonder how I can still be excited, or at any rate preoccupied, by economic, social and political problems since I know: (1) that we are going to die, (2) that revolution saves us neither from life nor from death, (3) that I cannot imagine a finite universe, an infinite universe, nor yet a universe that is neither finite nor infinite.

We are in life in order to die. Death is the aim of existence, that seems to be a commonplace truth. Sometimes, in a trite expression, the banality may vanish and truth appear, reappear, newborn. I am living through one of those moments when it seems to me that I am discovering for the first time that the only aim of existence is death. There's nothing we can do. There's nothing we can do. There's nothing we can do. But what sort of a puppet-like condition is this, what right have they to make a fool of me?

I still feel surprised, sometimes, that I'm no longer twelve years old.

On reading *Phaedo*, it's only towards the end of the dialogue that I realize what a fine mess we are in. Socrates has not managed to convince me that the soul is immortal and that he is going to live in a better world. You get the impression that Socrates' disciples are not convinced either, since they weep; otherwise, why should they weep? When evening comes and Socrates takes the poison, when his feet grow cold and then his stomach, when at last he dies, I am seized with terror and boundless unhappiness. The description of the death of Socrates is so convincing, far more convincing than his arguments for immortality. In any case, the arguments vanish in an instant; we forget them at once, but the image of Socrates dead is graven in my memory; all men are mortal, Socrates is a man, therefore Socrates is mortal. I lay awake last night thinking about this. For a long time I had not felt such lucid, vivid, glacial anguish. A fear of nothingness. How can I describe it? I clutched my breast to make sure that I was still there; then I suddenly had the sensation that the black nothingness had already begun to devour me and that I had lost my feet, my legs, my thighs; I was merely a torso, being consumed by the icy fire of nothingness. I put on the light. How good it is to be alive. I felt a surge of fondness for life, which seemed to me something miraculous, a luminous fairy tale springing out of the darkness. We kill one another because we know that we shall all be killed. It's out of hatred for death that we kill each other. Socrates' death, so peaceful and serene, seems to me quite improbable, and yet it is possible. But how?

It's impossible to understand anything about it. All those who fancy they do are fools. It's only when I say that everything is incomprehensible that I come as close as possible to understanding the only thing it is given to us to understand.

Nothing is mightier than our *why*, nothing stands above it, because in the end there is a *why* to which no answer is possible. In fact, from *why* to *why*, from one step to the next, you get to the end of things. And it is only by travelling from one *why* to the next, as far as the *why* that is unanswerable, that man attains the level of the creative principle, facing the infinite, equal to the infinite maybe. So long as he can answer the *why* he gets lost, he loses his way among things. 'Why this?' I answer, 'because that', and from one explanation to the next I reach the point where no explanation is satisfying, from one explanation to the next I reach zero, the absolute, where truth and falsehood are equivalent, become equal to one another, are identified with one another, cancel each other out in face of the absolute *nothing*. And so we can understand how all action, all choice, all history is justified, at the end of time, by a final cancelling-out. The *why* goes beyond everything. Nothing goes beyond the *why*, not even the *nothing*, because the *nothing* is not the explanation; when silence confronts us, the question to which there is no answer rings out in the silence. That ultimate *why*, that great *why* is like a light that blots out everything, but a blinding light; nothing more can be made out, there is nothing more to make out.

And yet it seems to me that through this unanswerable *why* I have gained a sort of advantage, if I can call it that, a sort of superiority over everything, even the One or the Deity, because neither It nor He can evade my questioning. Truth (plus) and Falsehood (minus) are mutually exclusive. It is my *why* that cancels them out. Nothing that has already happened or that is going to happen (Science, Progress, Evolution, Revolution, History) can surprise me any longer. It is as though I had nothing in front of me any more, as if everything lay behind me. In front of me I have nothing, not even *nothing*: everything has fled. 'Social' life has no meaning, no content. History appears to me as no more than a torrent of wrong answers, or answers that are partially true and absolutely false and useless.

I read a page of Plato's great work. I can no longer understand anything, because behind the words on the page, which have their own heavenly brightness, to be sure, there shines an even brighter, an enormous, dazzling *why* that blots out everything, cancels out, destroys all meaning. All individual intelligence. When one has understood, one stops, satisfied with what one has understood. *I do not understand.* Understanding is far too little. To have understood is to be fixed, immobilized. It's as though one wanted to stop on one step in the middle of a staircase, or with one foot in the void and the other on the endless stair. But a mere *why*, a new *why* can set one off again, can unpetrify what was petrified and everything starts flowing afresh. How can one 'understand'? One cannot.

(When I shall no longer exist, God will say: 'I do a lot of things that everybody understands. There's nobody left not to understand them.')

It's to Death, above all, that I say 'Why?' with such terror. Death alone can, and will, close my mouth.

Once, long ago, very long ago, it was with a sense of joy that I sat down at my desk to write. Next, it was merely with a certain pleasure. Later, it was with indifference, out of habit and even with a sort of boredom. Later still, when I was writing dozens of pages of a journal devoted to the arguments I had with my former friends who were becoming Fascists or Nazis or Iron Guards, I would sit down at my desk despite a certain reluctance. Today, the thought that I've got to write fills me with sheer horror. Today, when I begin to write, there stirs within me an even keener and more intolerable awareness of the tragedy, the danger, the universal anguish, and I long to escape, to divert my mind, to forget it all.

I am constantly waiting for things to change for the better: amid all the conflicting parties, I have chosen none. I am in the position of someone who hopes to win first prize in a lottery without having bought a ticket.

I am not sufficiently absorbed in the human comedy. I don't belong wholly to this world. I cannot quite detach myself from this world nor from the other. I am neither here nor there. Outside it all. I'm afraid of making a wrong choice, so I choose neither religion nor politics. The fear of failure is what makes one fail. If Grace should not come, that would be the *coup de grâce*.

In a dream I see a dog dying at the edge of the pavement. No, he's not dying, he has fainted. I saw him spit blood and urinate where he lay; I see him in a pool of blood and urine, breathing, coming back to life, and people going up to him. 'Don't stroke him,' I tell them, 'he's reviving, don't stroke him, it'll do him no good, don't stroke him, you'd soil your hands.'

Success is to the cunning, who bow to circumstances. They follow the main stream: so they always win. They win, but they don't exist, they have no being since they merely identify themselves with the stream; they adopt shapes, they are shapeless.

Some men find it so easy to live, they merely have to let themselves go. They drift. But I have to keep on scaling mountains, which in fact I never scale.

I am of the chosen race of those who have to attempt the impossible: I am also one of the laziest of my race: I stay where I am, and the mountains grow higher and more menacing. If I don't go towards the mountain, it will come towards me. I can already feel the earth quaking, I can see the terrible rocks about to fall on me and crush me.

I know, I renounce everything, but I don't renounce myself. One ought to do just the opposite.

My father used to come into my room when I was a schoolboy, to see if I had done my homework or to scold me for something or other. I'd get up, and I'd see him rummaging about everywhere, in my drawers, among my books. He would open my notebooks, read my most private diaries or my poems out loud. Flushed with anger, he would abuse me with mounting fury.

I should like to be able to tell a simple story, an idyll, a novella of about a hundred pages, a story with the Spring in it.

Works of art are living beings. I mean that they have a life as objective realities. The proof of this objective reality: the reactions they arouse are identical, and they are not meaningless reactions. I can foresee, too, what will be the subjective reactions of those who make contact with a work's objective reality. Since I can foresee them, this means that such subjectivity is objective, just as the objectivity is subjective. The value of a work lies in the fact that we perceive that it is identical with itself. The contact of its reality with my subjectivity makes no difference to it: the value of a work is defined by the strength and persistence of the impression it makes.

(Above all, I should like this to be the case. I am always afraid that a work may be only what we think it is, or rather what we want to think it is. In this case the work would be meaningless. *My* work would be meaningless.)

People talk a great deal about language nowadays, as if they had suddenly discovered that they had been talking for thousands and thousands of years. Now they are trying to find out what talking means. Deliberately or not, they are confusing the issue. Language is thought. It is also the manifestation of thought. It is at the same time thought and its manifestation. Language is one thing, ways of speaking are another. A way of speaking may be mere trickery; it should not be confused with language, which is certain.

Objectivity means being in harmony with one's own subjectivity, not lying to others or to oneself.

Both knowledge and creation, both revelation and discovery: communication and construction: the content and that which contains it: such is the work of art, which provides us with an endless flow of expressions, of images, of fresh aspects of the world. Ideologists benefit belatedly thereby.

The Crisis of Language

The divorce between thought and life. Thought, emptied of life, dries up, shrivels, is no longer thought. For thought is an expression of life, it is identical with life. One can speak without thinking; for this we have clichés, automatic expressions.

The only true thought is living thought.

Here is yet another life telling its story. Every life is unique. Every life is a whole universe. But no life means anything unless it reflects the universal life, unless it is at the same time itself and something else, it means nothing if it is separate, it means nothing, too, if it is lived gregariously, if it is lost in the nothingness of impersonality. To live one's life means experiencing the world in one's own fashion, in a different fashion, an unexpected fashion, like others and yet not unlike others.

So then I am the one who looks at himself (myself), a sort of impotent God. I am not only a watchful eye. I am also the one who experiences the passions, desires, and so forth, which are both myself and not myself, I am within, I am without: the one who makes, who is made, who sees what he does and how it is done, without really understanding.

My thought is something detached from myself. How is it

possible to be both here and there, how is thought possible? I think of myself: I am another. The 'I' is caught up in the 'myself'; its root is myself. My 'self' is the soil that feeds the 'I', it is its very sap.

If the universe does not belong to me, to whom does it belong? If I am not master of it, why am I not? how does it happen that the universe is not myself, why is it something different, myself on one side, everything else on the other? Everything is alien; I feel myself alien; and so are these thoughts, since they oppress me.

Everything is a burden. Is there anything that does not weigh on me?

I have a sort of impression that events are taking place within me, that things and passions are conflicting within me; that I am watching myself and seeing the struggle of these opposing forces, and that now one, now the other prevails; a mêlée, a mental battlefield, and that my real self is the 'I' who watches the 'myself' who am the scene of these happenings, these conflicts. I am not these passions, it seems, I am the one who beholds them, watches, comments, considers. I am also the one who yearns for a different self.

Without rhyme or reason.

I am not my passions, I am in my passions.

I cannot understand how it should be that for hundreds and hundreds and hundreds of years men have accepted life and death in these intolerable conditions: have accepted an existence haunted by the fear of death, amid war and pain, without showing any real, open, decisive reaction against it. How can mankind have put up with being here, having been flung here, with no explanation? We are caught in a sort of collective trap and we don't even rebel seriously against it. All philosophies, all sciences have proved unable to provide a key to the mystery. We are led by the nose, we are conditioned, we are dragged on a leash like dogs.

For tens of thousands of years man has been the victim of a hoax.

I am in it too, I am a man, and I have to accept the unacceptable: I don't want to make war, and I make war; I want to know, and I know nothing. If in the end I come to love this state of existence into which I have been plunged, I suffer because it is taken from me. I have certain powers, and they fail, I grow old and I don't want to grow old, I die and I don't want to die. This is the incredible thing: to love a life that has been thrust upon me and that is snatched away from me just when I have accepted it. There are old men of eighty who are happy to be alive: there are young men of twenty on whom the years weigh heavy. For thousands and thousands of years the same questions have been asked thousands of times, so often that it has become absurd to ask them again, they are worn out before we can find the slightest fragment of an answer. Men are beginning to know a little bit of the universe, the earth has been photographed from the moon, we know the laws of physics and the chemical consitution of the cosmos; we still have only a few faint gleams to light up the profound darkness of our psyche; we can see through flesh, we can disintegrate matter, of course, we can foresee the movements of the stars, of course, of course, and so many other things, of course, of course. Science is not knowledge, rhetoric and philosophy are nothing but words, sets of words, strings of words, but words are not speech. When we have learnt everything, or if we could learn everything, we should still know nothing. What sets it all in motion? What is the life behind things? The universe appears to me as merely a storehouse of objects in disorderly, or perhaps in orderly array, mobile objects flung into the immensity of space, but who flung them, and what is that which I call space, which appears to me as space? But even if I know what governs their trajectory, if I know the rules of the movement of things and how things are organized and how certain mutations, transformations, gestations take place, even if I know all that, I shall only have learnt how to get along after a fashion in the enormous gaol, the oppressive prison in which I am held. What a farce, what a snare, what a booby-trap. We were born cheated. For if we are not to know, if there is nothing to know, why do we have this longing to know?

I can know the laws; I cannot know the reason for the laws. Why is it that we can't know everything, can't be everywhere at once? What is there behind the walls? Why don't the limits of my understanding break down, so that I can understand everything, so that it can all become familiar and natural to me, as it should? The fact that the world, distances, nature seem to me unnatural, strange, improbable, terrifying, that's just what is improbable, unnatural and terrifying. Are my desires myself, am I made up of them, or have they been superimposed on me from elsewhere, and in that case what is the 'I' that receives them? I am what I think, what I desire, what I feel. But in that case are epidemics part of the people they attack, does my sickness create me or do I create my sickness, and what is this 'I' that thinks it thinks, that may perhaps be nothing at all and yet, being nothing, thinks it thinks? Most of the thoughts and ideas that dwell in me come from outside me, from anywhere outside me; I should still have been 'I' if I had never had them; 'I' am a crossroads, a meeting-place for universal forces and wills of whose essential nature I shall for ever remain ignorant.

This 'I' ought to give up, it ought to abdicate. One should let oneself go. 'I' am prevented from letting myself go; desires surge up against my will, an anxious self thwarts my serene self, which self is really me? I want to know. I feel impelled to know. I cannot prevent myself from wanting to know. I am not master of my desires or my depressions or my anguish. Or else my anguish, my longings, my distress are a self that refuses to be serene. Is my anguish an alien self or is it myself?

Let us accept empirical awareness. I assume that 'I' exist and that I am myself.

I assert that learning is useless. I assert that science can never get to the essence of our being. I don't care if I know nothing, for learning is 'mundane', and I am not interested in such things: what takes place, what's done, what moves. I am not interested in the mechanism of our movements, not at all; what lies behind, the Unknown, He or It, is alone worthy of our interest. Knowledge, not learning. Knowledge is impossible. But I cannot resign myself to knowing only the walls of my prison.

Strictly speaking, perhaps, there are no such things as the conscious and unconscious mind. In dream I am conscious only with another sort of consciousness. In dream, either I know that I am dreaming or else, if I don't know it, what appears to me is none the less the obverse side of things, or their depth; one sees things from within; the view is quite different. It's as though one were not looking down at things from above but looking up at them from below, as if one were at the bottom of an abyss between mountain sides and could see all the way up to the mountain top and the sky. It's at night, in dream, that you can see the sky most clearly. Dreams are said to be revealing, and since the latest psychologists have taught us more precisely how, everyone admits this—of course they are, but they speak through ciphers, that's to say they show and at the same time they conceal what they show; what a dream reveals, breaking through censorships and by means of symbols, is what the waking consciousness hides. The waking consciousness reveals what the language of the dream seeks to hide. The dream tears off the mask. The waking consciousness is governed by passions. It does not allow us to know what are the deep reasons for human actions and thoughts. It is the surface of things. We can construct systems of philosophy, ideologies, we can have all kinds of thoughts without knowing where they come from, or why. But of course this consciousness serves the needs of surface realism, practical life, techniques. Dream consciousness, in its turn, needs to be elucidated, interpreted by the waking consciousness. So that in fact there really seem to be two aspects of consciousness, or two sorts of consciousness, one reflected in the other, one explaining the other, two consciousnesses unmasking one another. I incline to think, however, that the language of dream is more luminous than the other, what it expresses contains an unquestionable, living truth; everyday thinking stays more on the outside of things. It does not express their inner core.

The Society I try to describe in a play like *The Bald Primadonna* is a perfect society, that's to say one where all administrative, economic and political problems have been solved. It's when this point has been reached that the basic problems can arise. Politics— by which I mean all our worries, major or minor, more or less urgent—concealed these from us. What can we do when our worries have disappeared? Without worries, boredom ensues. But where there is not even boredom, there is spiritual degeneration.

The Society sought by revolutionary economists seems to me a two-dimensional one. They propel us towards social conformism, the world of alienation, the world that deprives man of his third dimension. From this point of view the so-called Socialist world has shown itself, hitherto, more alienating than the bourgeois world.

I have always felt ill at ease in my own body; hence my need for drink, for euphoric stimulants. . . .

If only one could let oneself live, let oneself go, drift on the stream of existence, let oneself live and thus, perhaps, manage to let oneself die, offering the least resistance!

(These are mere words, powerless, useless.)

Indifference, hostility, mistrust are states of disgrace.

Love is a state of grace. . . . Calmness or resignation, the hardest thing to attain.

A dream: I find myself in a very dark house, immense rooms, I can't even make out the walls; are they really rooms, or am I in the forest? To master my anguish, I eat large pieces of bread. But this dark yet wall-less house, this open palace stands on a mountain top. I try to go down. People dressed in black are waiting for me in the valley, where there is a village. I go down. Just before I reach the bottom I see these people, I see little low houses, half buried in the ground. Then I go uphill again. I can't feel at ease anywhere; in either place, a threat hangs over me. But they are two different sorts of threat; I cannot define them. I only know that the threat I feel down below is different from the one I feel up above. . . .

Above all, one must not let oneself disintegrate; one must endure, resist, keep on living. . . .

Soon death, or old age. I have always dreaded that. Probably

35

from the day of my birth I have been unwilling to wait for it, to accept it, I have dreaded it.

Should one envy the dead, who have nothing more to fear? ... Have they nothing more to fear? I take refuge in life as in a precarious shelter; I would rather go on dreading. Three of my friends have rounded the cape.

What is the name of the character in Brecht's *Dreigroschenoper* of whom someone else says that he is only a filthy little bourgeois because, of course, he kills, but is not fond of killing *when it's not necessary*? So one has to learn to kill gratuitously and cheerfully, one ought also to discover the pleasure of killing. Jean Genêt, too, wants men to discover this delight. In his play *The Blacks*, he teaches us that black men must enjoy killing whites.

Revolutionary ideologies are more hypocritical: they provide a justification for murder, an invented moral code for murder, an invented 'historical necessity' to vindicate it.

I keep beginning again. I keep taking a fresh notebook. And each time I hope that it will lead to something, that it will be a constructive experiment, that I shall open some door. It never happens. I stop before I get to a door, any door. The same invisible obstacle; if it were visible I should skirt round it. It's the invisible that stops me. I ought at least to try to keep to the same notebook, to get to the last page. That would mean that I'd have said almost everything. It's all the things I still have to say that make up the obstacle, the invisible barriers that block my way. There's no open space within me; I cannot even reach my own door, nor the window to let in a little air.

Today the great majority of Negroes in Africa and in certain great centres of the United States have no longer any *economic* reason for hostility towards white men, it is merely a question of wounded pride, of humiliation; the Yellow races, particularly the Chinese, hate the Whites for the same reason; the Whites were more powerful and conquered them; theirs is a centuries-old humiliation. In many so-called socialist countries the former owners were deprived of what they formerly owned. But hatred persisted; a new racism set in: people were hated not because they were White, Black, Yellow or Jewish, but because they were bourgeois, or sons or grandsons of bourgeois, they were hated for having, not what the Nazis called an unhealthy ethnic origin, but an unhealthy social origin; in fact it comes to the same thing; in certain socialist countries, until quite recently, children of bourgeois families did not have the right to university education; these bourgeois children were like Negro children in the Southern states of America; racial hatred, which is not even social hatred and has nothing to do with socialism, is always the fruit of wounded pride.

Marx was wrong; jealousy and pride, emotional forces, are just as responsible as hunger and economic necessity for our actions; they explain the whole of History, and the initial fall of man. The authors of the Bible were in possession of a psychological truth that is both fundamental and universal.

I have just re-read certain chapters of *The Decline of the West*. Spengler was wrong. I am naturally pessimistic or mistrustful in metaphysical matters. Yet I cannot fail to notice that the universal History which Spengler called in question is now being realized, amid, and despite, these manifold catastrophes. He believed, as we know, in separate races, nations or communities, each living its own life as an autonomous and individual organism.

Nor, perhaps, is Art about to vanish, although he predicted its imminent end. Art, it seems, persists in proving itself an essential and permanent function. Between races or civilizations, between ethnic groups, so Spengler thought, there are insuperable barriers. Modern methods of communication are bringing these barriers down, despite persistent opposition from Russia and China, despite the paradoxical patriotism of those whose aim was once to promote internationalism. In short, the barriers are crumbling, thanks to cosmopolitanism. Unity is in sight.

It is surprising that Spengler completely failed to foresee that the struggle for the 'imperium mundi' was not to be between America, England, Germany and Russia. He had not foreseen the collapse of Germany. He had not foreseen the weakening of England. He had not foreseen the new imperialisms: China, very soon the united Arabs, soon perhaps South America and in the near future Africa, later on India. He had some curious myths; he believed in the ineluctable ageing of countries. But countries die and then are reborn from their ashes. Biologically, France, which he thought doomed, has been regenerated, its birth-rate and its economy are progressing. Nations are intermingling. This explains the possibility of unity in spite of the conflict of imperialisms.

I note other assertions which seem to me more than questionable. The Greeks, he says, had no sense of duration, they lacked any awareness of historical change, their mental universe was static, and they projected this static quality on to the external world. And yet Thucydides, Herodotus and Xenophon related events of the past, events which had taken place *before*; they created History. To be sure, the Greeks conceived of archetypes; Aristotle and Plato, above all, bear witness to this. But they had, before ourselves, before anyone else, the sense of History, of duration, of the process of becoming, of Time, which bears everything away. Witness Heraclitus, who 'never swam twice in the same river'. And if modern thinkers sometimes attain a sense of duration or a historical view of the world it's because when they cease to be Platonists they follow Heraclitus. He undoubtedly inspired Hegel and Bergson.

It is just because the Greeks were conscious of the immutability of archetypes that, inevitably, they were also conscious of mutability; Lupasco explains this very clearly. For surely nothing can exist in our minds except by contrast with its opposite, which also exists but is repressed.

André Breton's mistake was perhaps to have taken himself too seriously. One must take oneself a little seriously, otherwise one would lack substance altogether, e.g. Alphonse Allais. But if you take yourself too seriously, liberty vanishes; you are a prisoner, you cannot breathe, your movements are constricted, you can't stir, you're caught, you're stuck to things, you can't get far enough back to see. One must be partly serious.

I was a student, and I was twenty. Several of us were sitting round a table drinking. One friend of mine, Stéphane M., was still a student at twenty-seven, being in no hurry to finish his studies. 'If I become a schoolmaster at twenty-seven instead of twenty-five, or at thirty or even at thirty-five, what difference can it make? Instead of being a teacher for forty years I shall be one for thirty. Thirty or forty, it all comes to the same. I'd rather enjoy myself while I still feel young enough.' He began to sing a drinking-song about youth decked in fine new clothes and old age in heavy shabby garments. We parted in the middle of the night. I went to bed and dreamed that I was old and bent, that time weighed heavy on me, that I was sixty. I woke up in acute distress. It was spring-time, the sky was blue and the sun was shining. Oh, I'm only twenty, I said to myself with relief.

Now, at fifty, the dream has almost come true. How can I accept this situation, how can one consent to go on living, bearing the heavy weight of time, like an ass's burden? It's beyond all endurance. One ought to revolt. I'm like a schoolboy at the end of the holidays.

I remember something that happened years and years ago. We were completely destitute of money, and I had beside me a big packet of envelopes into which I had to slip prospectuses and on which I had to write addresses; I was already living by my pen. The sun was overcast; I was waiting for a break in the clouds. Then, suddenly, it came. The table, the carpet, the old sofa, the whole room was suddenly flooded with light. The old carpet looked beautiful in the sudden golden light. The furniture was new again. The sun shone on the castle, the trees, the river and bridge in the worn tapestry hanging on the wall. The world was transformed. I was steeped in light, my whole self transfigured from within.

I was at the same time rooted in myself and detached from myself, as if I were both the actor and the spectator of myself. I could watch myself existing, in the June light. 'We are very poor, darling,' I said to her, 'but nothing matters just now except this radiant light of Being which is our bread and our wine.'

I often suffer from insomnia. I open my eyes in the darkness. But this darkness is like an unfamiliar brightness, a negative light.

And this black brightness brings me, with a certainty beyond question, 'the revelation of disaster, of catastrophe, of failure irremediable and absolute'. There is nothing left.

Childhood is the world of miracle and wonder: as if creation rose, bathed in light, out of the darkness, utterly new and fresh and astonishing. The end of childhood is when things cease to astonish us. When the world seems familiar, when one has got used to existence, one has become adult. The brave new world, the wonderland has grown trite and commonplace. That was our true Paradise, that was how the world was on the first day. Losing one's childhood means losing Paradise, becoming adult. You retain the memory, the longing for a present, a presentness, a plenitude that you try to recover by all possible means; to recover it, or to compensate for it. I have been, I still am tormented at once by the dread of death, the horror of the void, and by an eager, impatient, urgent desire to live. Why does one long to live, what does living mean? I have waited for life. A longing to live does not mean seeking to regain the sense of wonder which is accessible only to childhood or to minds of great innocence and lucidity; failing this, one yearns to be fully satisfied. And this one never is, and can never be. The good things of life are not life. One never succeeds in living. 'Longing to live' means nothing. I had sought salvation on the wrong road, I had gone astray.

I have found some pages of an old diary, dating from . . . no matter; so long ago that I feel dizzy. I had published scarcely anything, I had written no plays, perhaps a few scraps of dialogue. I had the same problems; I have always had the same problems. And today I am as incapable as I was then, as I ever was, of giving any answers. I have solved nothing; I am still questioning. It's when I am fully conscious that I ask questions. Otherwise it's mere oblivion, the sleep of the mind. Here, then, are these pages:

I sometimes wake up, become conscious, realize that I am surrounded by things and by people, and if I look closely at the sky or the wall or the earth or the hand writing or not writing, I have the impression that I'm seeing it all for the first time. Then, as if it were the first time, I wonder, or I ask, 'What's that?' I look all round me and I ask, 'What are all these things? where am I? who

40

am I? what do these questions mean?' And then sometimes a sudden light, a great blinding light floods over everything, obliterates all meanings, all our preoccupations, all those shadows, that's to say all those walls that makes us imagine limits, distinctions, separations, significances. I can no longer even ask myself a question like: 'What is society?' because I cannot go beyond the first, the fundamental question, beyond that blinding, burning light that springs from one's questioning and that is so strong that it contains everything, consumes everything, dissolves everything away. Only an intense love quite without object could resist the blinding light of one's questioning, and that intense love is transformed, enhanced, becomes an irrational euphoria that seems to set the universe on fire.

It is natural that things should appear, or be manifest, because they are. Essence is a perfectly sufficient and satisfactory explanation for existence. If a thing is, it must also logically exist. What I cannot succeed in understanding is this: How can anything be? Why something is? It would be more 'natural', if I may use the word, for nothing to be. For the whole thing not to be. For nothing ever to have been. Of course it is inconceivable that nothing should be, that there should be nothing. I try to conceive the inconceivable: I suddenly picture a kind of solid whole, compact and absurdly full. Not to be, that there should be no being, is impossible and absurd; to be is equally absurd, though 'possible'. Why is there what there is, why does what is there appear as it does, why isn't there something different, why are things as they are? Everything is there, all the time, and it's exhausting.

I felt that everything was emptying away. I was not conscious of this as an emptiness devouring my being, holding me captive, I myself being reduced to a kind of framework round the void, and gradually being consumed and absorbed by nothingness. It was not that familiar sense of heavy emptiness, if I may use such an expression. This time it was like a release, things lost their weight around me, I was cutting adrift from things and they were losing all arbitrary, conventional significance, all that enormous mass of meanings of all sorts, contradictory, intricate meanings amidst which I had been trapped, that labyrinth of tangled paths in which I had lost my way. Everything was now pervaded by a dazzling light, and as I became aware, with limitless joy, that everything exists, I could think of nothing else but this: everything exists, all things exist; and I became aware that their existence was transfigured, that they existed quite differently, in a heavenly light, delicate, fragile.

Fragility seemed to be one of the qualities of Appearance, of Manifestation. And yet this fragility was not disturbing; quite the contrary. A great luminous energy seemed for ever on the point of breaking things up, of dissolving them; and this light, this force seemed to have been hidden under the mask of things, and now it was bursting forth, exploding. A light like no other: things had been particular incidents within this light, the incident-objects through which it assumed specific shape. In fact it had only been on the point of exploding and dissolving everything; the fire had not spread. Things had become luminous, translucent, but their contours had only been on the point of fading and vanishing, there had been no ecstasy, no sense of union or unification. None the less I seemed to have come to some frontier, the extreme limit of history, yet not beyond it. Why had this flood of light stopped short? Why had I myself not caught fire in the universal conflagration? Who, within myself, had halted everything, what accident, what error had frustrated everything? It seemed as though the luminous energy had met with some invisible obstacle, lighter than a cloud, a haze of smoke drifting over everything, blackening everything. In one instant things became once again heavy, opaque and dark; I understood, from that moment, that things are beautiful only in so far as they retain a little of that light. I myself seemed to grow heavy again, dense, heavy as lead, a mere thing, a leaden thing that emptiness can eat away.

I feel none the less that I had been at the frontier of existence, close to the place where things lose their name, their definition, the place where time stops, almost outside History.

I have had that experience, I have felt what it is to be outside History. A man can get there. That state of primitive astonishment, of stupefaction is intrinsic to mankind and can illuminate any man, irrespective of his social status, his historical time, his economic condition. None of these qualifications play any part here, none contributes to the birth of this experience or its disappearance. It took place, it still takes place in that sort of no-man's-land on the border of the absolute or of nothingness. Anyone, in the twentieth century as in the fifteenth or in any other century, be he a husbandman of Biblical times or a petit bourgeois of today, can once or twice in his life experience this, can be pervaded by this luminous, irresistible sense of wonder, he can have that feeling of the supreme strangeness of the universe which is a-historical and fundamentally a-social. And I wonder if this strange feeling, this unanswerable and almost unquestioning astonishment is not the deepest reaction of my consciousness. More truly, I don't wonder; I know that this astonishment is indeed my most authentic consciousness. I know that the answer lies in the very impossibility of answering. Silence is the best answer.

Exit the King

Here are some pages from a journal I kept five or six years ago, or some notes for *Exit the King*, which I was about to start writing. These fragments of dialogue were not inserted into the text of the play.

★

THE QUEEN SPEAKS: If you love me, you should be willing to grow old along with me. We were together in youth, we are together in old age. I should be glad to grow old by your side. Alas, you love yourself better than you love me. You made a vow to love me, to grow old with me, to die with me. You are not strong enough to keep it, you are not brave enough, because you have not love enough. You want to break your promise. You want to desert your destiny.

★

Not to get bogged down in reality.

★

THE QUEEN: How could you get so rooted in this world? you cling to it, you believe in the world, you dig your nails into these clouds, this unreal stuff which you take for reality, for rock. You see, it's giving way, it's breaking up, it's dissolving into clouds, flakes, snow, water, steam, smoke. You cling to it. . . . Try to loosen your hold, little by little. . . . Break the habit of living. How could you forget that all this is just a brief passage? you used to know that, you said you knew it. But you can't have known it. You were lying to yourself. You knew without really knowing.

★

'You are a shipwrecked sailor, lost at sea, you call out, there's no one to hear you, you make signals, you wave your arms, your handkerchief. Keep still. Nobody can see you, nobody can hear you.

'Or else, it's worse. . . . The lifeboats pass by you. The men look

44

at you from the deck. They won't come to save you. They won't come to help you. Your cries, your tears, your despair are all in vain. They don't care. When their turn comes, the same thing will happen to them.'

*

THE QUEEN: You are lying on the pavement, in the street. . . . There's a crowd of people hurrying by. They think they are going somewhere, but they don't really know where they are going. You cry out. They step aside so as not to crush you, for they aren't cruel, just indifferent. They each carry their own death within them, they cannot carry yours as well. . . .

*

THE EXECUTIONER TO THE KING: I'll have to pull you away from there, if you won't let go yourself, if you can't loosen your hold. It'll hurt you even more, but what else can I do, if that's the only way? If you won't make a start yourself?

THE KING: Help me to die. But not you. No, nor you. No, not you either. (*To the Beauty.*) Nor you either, above all not you. I will try by myself.

*

They ask him: 'You haven't always been alive; what were you before, where were you before? Were you in infinite Time? The Universe got on very well without you.'

Juliette says: 'You got on quite well before you were alive, you got on far better.'

They say to him: 'Do you remember the blackness, the abyss, the blackness, the nothingness, the unfathomable depths? Do you remember?

'It's only the living who imagine that death, nothingness, is a sort of night.

'Nothingness is not heavy. Nothing could be lighter. It is lightness itself. . . . Why, you're scarcely born; ten minutes later you never want to die.'

*

Children die more easily. Very easily. They have not taken root, they are not established, they have as yet no instinct of self-preservation. We form deplorable habits. Turn back, become a child again to meet death.

45

A guide is taking visitors or tourists round the Throne Rooms, or showing them a white funeral monument.

THE GUIDE: Ladies and gentlemen, boys and girls, ten minutes ago our great King Bérenger was living here. . . . A hundred years ago, our great King Bérenger lived here. . . . Ten thousand years ago, a great king called Bérenger lived here with his court. . . . It is said that twenty thousand years ago men were already civilized and lived under a king whose name was said to be Bérenger. . . . Ladies and gentlemen, according to legend there was once a palace here in which a king lived. Archaeologists have dug the site. But in fact nobody ever lived here. The place has always been a desert.

*

Didn't you yourself say that man is made to die, that he must serve his apprenticeship to death? . . . And that when you attained a certain age you would prepare yourself for it? That age has come and gone, and have you started training?

*

'No. . . . Not yet.'
'It's high time.'
'I need years, a brief respite. An hour and a half is too short.'
'It's quite time enough, there's always time, hurry up. . . . Let's try together.'
'Ten minutes longer, Mr Executioner, one minute longer, Mr Executioner, just thirty seconds longer.'

*

THE QUEEN: Don't you feel a slight weariness? . . . a slight lassitude? that's the beginning. Give way to your weariness, relax in your weariness, sink deeper into your lassitude, savour your lassitude. Come on, let yourself drift away.

THE KING: Save me, stop me from falling. I want to drift gently, pausing to take breath from time to time. Don't leave go of the ropes. I'm so dizzy, I'm afraid of the precipice. . . .

*

THE EXECUTIONER TO THE KING: If your Majesty refuses to die, I shall be obliged to wrench you out of life, and it will be like pulling out a large molar without an anaesthetic. It'll be very painful, it would be pleasanter or at least easier to flutter down gently like a dead leaf dropping from a branch.

46

'Today or tomorrow, it all comes to the same thing, surely? If it were left to you, you'd never make up your mind.'

*

THE KING: When I say *enough*, when I say it of my own accord.

THE QUEEN: You'd never say it.

THE KING: Yes, I might, perhaps. If everyone else had died before me, if I were the last survivor, if I was bored from spending hundreds and hundreds of years alone in a deserted universe. If I was very, very ill. If I was a widower. If I was in love and my beloved had died. If I was in love with nobody in particular and there was nobody for me to love. If perhaps I was feeling very ill, if I was very cold, if I had nothing left but memories, if all my memories were sinking away, fading away one after the other and there was nothing left but an abyss of oblivion. . . . When I shall have forgotten my name, my kingdom, my wives, who I am, who I was. . . . Then, perhaps, if I should still be lucid enough to say *enough*, I'll be ready to die. Or else when the world has changed so much that men seem like unfamiliar monsters, when I am even more afraid to go on living than to die.

THE EXECUTIONER: That would take too long. Or else it would never happen.

THE KING: Don't be in such a hurry, wait a little longer. Let's discuss it, let me explain. I have to take care of this kingdom as long as there's still one living person in it. I have to supply his needs. The king must be the last to die. What would a subject do on earth without his King?

THE EXECUTIONER: Stop joking, your Majesty. It's very late.

THE KING: I won't. (*He struggles, he runs away, the Executioner seizes him, flings him on to the throne and holds him there, almost prostrate.*)

THE QUEEN TO THE EXECUTIONER: Stop. I'll help him to make an easier end. There's quite a ceremony about it. We've got to keep to the conventions. Nobody knows quite why. Apparently they serve some purpose.

*

(Is there a universal consciousness? Is consciousness all-pervading? Is there a dormant consciousness in stone, as I believe

47

Leibnitz thought? Neither Planck, nor Heisenberg, nor Einstein, nor de Broglie wholly reject the idea of a universal, cosmic consciousness. There may be some plan, some intention. If there is an intention, there is consciousness. These thinkers do not exclude the idea of a God who would be that consciousness.)

*

THE KING: Let go, did you say? Nobody, nothing lets go willingly. A stone resists the pickaxe, wood resists when you split or break it; everything resists, fights back, defends itself, everything holds on and persists in holding on. A rat or an ant is terrified of death, fleas defend themselves, and microbes, everything that exists would rather kill than be killed. Everything clings to its own integrity. Everything seeks to devour the rest of the world, cankers spread, armies crush whole nations and put the conquered to the sword; they all want to take everything and give nothing . . . to destroy others and preserve themselves. Giving is the beginning of death. Oh, if only molecules could separate from one another of their own free will! It's the cohesion of my molecules that is responsible for my anguish. If only I could find out where the stitches are, take myself to pieces, undo the ligatures as one unties a knot of string! If I were unfastened, it would be easy. How can I untie this knot, how can I give up my will; or else will myself to be like water that can be poured into any vessel, thrown to the winds . . . or a vapour, or the wind; these are things that seem to suffer less than others when they disintegrate, there are no knots in them. But I am made up of tight knots, knots that resist, that insist on being knots. I cannot, I will not, I cannot, I will not.

*

She says: 'Shall we be together on the other side? I won't let death part us. There's got to be another side, there's absolutely got to be one, so that we can be together.'

*

Sometimes life seems so beautiful. One is tempted to say thank you to Providence. But one mustn't; it's better to sulk. Perhaps Providence likes those who sulk; she tries to cajole them.

*

For *The King*.

'Light!' says the King (and the stage grows dark).

Then the walls fade away. The stage lights up at the end (but I chose a different ending).

*

THE SECOND QUEEN, either lying to the King or speaking a truth in which she dares not believe herself: 'We shall soon have a second wedding. Nothing will be lost. Everything will be recovered, I swear to you, we cannot possibly lose, since we resent losing.'

Or else: 'You won't walk again, you won't move again, you won't see again, you won't hear again, yet you'll feel yourself surrounded by limitless, endless love. We are made for joy.'

*

Perhaps I shall keep on to the end writing books and plays, because I can't do anything but that. I'm incapable of any other profession. Since I've known myself, I have never done anything else.

Knocks

I felt the first knock. It bent me. I felt the second knock. It did not break me. Then came the third knock. Next the fourth. Then came the fifth knock. Next came the sixth knock. Then came the seventh knock. Next came the eighth knock. Then came the ninth knock. Next came the tenth knock, a hard one. Then came the eleventh knock, even harder. They came crashing down on all sides. Suddenly I felt the thirteenth knock, followed by the fourteenth. Then came the fifteenth, after that the sixteenth. Then came the seventeenth. After that the eighteenth. Then came the nineteenth knock. After that came the twentieth. At the twenty-first, I stopped my watch.

According to Freud, the three obstacles that prevent us from being free are anxiety, pity and aversion. This is the threefold chain that binds us. We know, furthermore, that psychoanalysis includes no moral judgment. Things are like that, and that's all. We must simply know why they are like that, why they have got to this point. Psychoanalysis enlightens but does not judge. Psychoanalysis moreover explains why we pass judgment, but passes no judgment on our judgment either.

But our chain is fourfold or even fivefold: hatred or aggressiveness are equal hindrances to freedom. It might perhaps be said that hatred is merely an intensification of aversion. Desire is the most serious obstacle to our deliverance. Freudianism can thus, to some extent, be reconciled with Buddhism. Not with Zen, for to wish to free oneself is still a form of will. One should seek to free oneself from wishing, to attain the state when one no longer even wishes to free oneself.

The connection between Buddhism and the thought of Freud seems to me all the more convincing because Freud himself, towards the end of his life, discovered and asserted that we have within us, that our whole being bears within itself a death instinct, a longing for rest, the 'Nirvana instinct', in the words of the great analyst himself.

Desire, or Eros, keeps us alive. If we succeeded in shedding light on Desire, stripping the mystery from Desire and all our desires, that's to say from all particular manifestations of Desire, from the reasons, the secrets of Desire or of our desires, then Desire would disappear. If we could learn the real reasons for our reasons, there would no longer be any reason for anything. All knots would be slackened, we would surrender ourselves and lapse into indifference and nothingness. Indifference would, moreover, allow us to live, that's to say it might make life less unendurable. Not longing to live, not longing to die, just letting things drift. Zen, or a metaphysical 'couldn't-care-less' attitude; the ultimate implications of psychoanalysis are not far removed from Zen.

Before learning how neither to live nor to die, the immediate problem facing me is learning how to die. This I have set myself. This is the moment, the last possible moment. What an undertaking! Before me a huge wall, a cliff impossible to scale. It's vastly beyond my strength, today at any rate. And yet my duty is to climb over it, or else to pass through it. My deepest feeling bids me do so, if I'm to believe my dreams. And what else is one to believe, if not what dreams tell one; they are the expression of one's innermost thoughts. To say that when you dream you are not conscious is to speak loosely; one is only conscious, only lucid in dream. Thus I found myself in the middle of a square surrounded by ruined houses, dingily grey. This square was just a piece of waste ground, full of withered brushwood and dry shrivelled thistles with no flowers. My wife was at my right hand. Before me rose up an enormous church, or rather the very high wall of a sort of church, a wall almost as broad as it was high; like the wall of a great prison. On the right, low down, a tiny door, closed. The wall of the church, which was a blackish grey, was pitted with small holes of a lighter grey. Now it looked like a great vertical graveyard seen from a distance, as it might appear to a bird, except for being upright.

On the left of this wall, on the left facing me, a kind of very high tower surmounted by a baroque cupola perched on pillars between which, on all four sides, I can glimpse the sky, or rather an empty space, dreary and wan. 'You told me the church was beautiful. You see that's not true. It's very ugly, on the contrary,' my wife says, adding: 'I noticed that before you did. Besides, it's Maurice's opinion too, and he knows about such things.'

We go left to skirt the building. Under the tower there's a sort of passage leading to a grimy kitchen, with holes in the walls letting through the same wan light that I'd noticed at the top of the tower.

In front of the left-hand wall stands the black figure of an old woman: the cook, in her black apron, in front of the blackened wall on which hang kitchen utensils that are equally black. We pass through the kitchen and find ourselves in a sloping field covered with the same tangled, withered vegetation, under the same drab sky.

'The X-ray reveals that you have had cancer of the heart. You were told your backaches were due to arthritis. This was untrue. The fact is that you have really had cancer. But it has been re-absorbed and has now healed.'—'Tell me the truth, doctor, you're a friend of mine, you mustn't lie to me. I'm capable of facing the truth.'—'All right, I'll tell you everything, but watch out, I'm going to tread on your toes.' (An odd expression, but that was how he put it.) 'Since you really want to know, you've not had cancer, you've got it now.' I try to master my panic. 'Here are the actual X-rays,' the doctor says. 'That curved shape distorting the lower end of the heart, that's where the cancer is. See for yourself!' I look at the heart, a black shadow shaped like a pear with its stalk end curving sideways. Round the heart a darkish space in which one can make out little pale scars or scratches look-ing like those small white pieces of whalebone that are used to stiffen shirt-collars. I make a great effort to conceal my anguish, for there are several people sitting round me and I feel ashamed. And she is there, among those people; a lighter, paler figure than the rest. She sits with her legs crossed, on a stool, smoking a cigarette, and seems uninterested in my terror. I ask the doctor: 'How long can one live with cancer of the heart?'—'Two or three months, or two or three years, it depends on the individual's vitality.'—'More likely two months than two years,' I told my-self. 'One can't live longer than that with cancer, particularly of the heart. I'd planned to learn how to die; alas, I've started too late. I shall never have time. It takes at least two or three years to learn about death, to loosen one's ties.'

Z., to whom I told this dream, said to me that my dread of dy-ing concealed something else. He pointed out to me that the heart in the dream—which he made me draw—seemed to have been squeezed out of shape by some hand grasping it tightly. And it is the inability to escape from the hand that grips one, inhibits one, prevents one's aggressiveness—which is one's life—from finding an outlet, that gives rise to this extreme, this mortal anxiety.

I am in a kind of translucent packing-case, possibly made of plastic, in the midst of interplanetary space; I am sitting in it with my legs stretched out, naked, tiny, the size of a five- or six-year-old child; in front of me is another child, in the same position, who looks like my twin; is he my double? Around this closed case lies the boundless dark chaos of cosmic space, its dark colours subtly shaded.

We come to the end of our journey. I don't think I was aware, while in the box, of where we were going. And now we've reached our goal: I am on another planet. I am an adult now, but very young. I am always young in my dreams, between sixteen and twenty-two or -three. Why? According to my interpretation, for two reasons (1) because I refuse to grow old and die and because I still feel obliged to be very formal and well-mannered with anyone over the age of forty, feeling that he must be older than myself, whence my sense of non-communication with people of my own age or slightly younger, whom I consider to belong to an older generation, though this does not prevent me from feeling equally out of touch with young people, who also belong to a different generation; but for as long as I can remember I have never been able to communicate with the young, especially when I was young myself. (2) Furthermore, I am seventeen in my dreams because it was at that age that all my problems about existence and knowledge were first clearly formulated and began to trouble me, and because they are still there, still unsolved, for how can one find any solution for fundamental problems such as: what's the meaning of birth, of old age, of death; why am I here, why am I surrounded by all these things that I look at with an astonishment that I have never shed, that is as new as on the day my consciousness first emerged? What, why? I keep on asking. We can solve nothing except practical problems; that's enough for most people, who never worry about first causes, or rather about the origin of things, nor about ultimate ends; our science, our technique, our activity provide merely external, secondary solutions; if we were made otherwise our enormous technical progress would have diminished and not increased our anxiety, our aggressiveness, our fury, that irrational and therefore deep-seated discontent, unleashed under cover of ideology, all of which conceal the essential problem, conceal us from ourselves, settle nothing but on the contrary seem likely to blow up the whole works.

Here I am then on another planet; we get off at a crowded little station. Crowded with people. I see a motor-coach full of travellers, among them a one-eyed man with a black patch over his left eye, and a man with a black beard. I leave the station with a companion, that unknown companion of one's dreams who may perhaps be one's other self, one's severe, critical self. I walk with this companion down the streets of this other planet, down a broad avenue like the Boulevard Lefevre in Paris. I feel terribly anxious. I talk to my companion. It looks as if we won't be able to get back to earth. What will become of us? They say there'll be machines to take us home. I don't believe it. They've not invented a way. This is where we're going to die. I long for earth and its graveyards. We're done for. My companion scolds me for my lack of courage. He sends me back to the station to get return tickets to the earth, or rather tickets for excursions round this planet with the people in the coach, whose guide he seems to be. At the booking-office a short dark woman who reminds me of my mother speaks to me in Italian. I don't know Italian. It's the language they speak on this planet. I leave the station to ask one of my fellow-travellers who knows Italian to help me make myself understood. I can't find any of them. I am separated from them by the crowd, I am alone amid a crowd of strangers, hurrying by uncaring; a crowd of people belonging to another planet. I am seized with infinite anguish; everything is grey and gloomy.

Z. tells me that my dreams are archetypal. The wall is an archetype; the box, travelling through space, in which I am shut up in an almost foetal position, is equally archetypal.

'Your distress in your dream is due to having left the earth. Earth, as you know, means the mother.'

'Since dreams are true, at least we know what to expect. The Martians speak Italian; that's worth knowing!'

The dread, the panic that seizes me at nightfall; I long for solitude and yet I cannot stand it. A matter of habit, perhaps. I think of the two of them, and I'm afraid for their sake. Night falls, it falls on my back, or rather I sink into it. Boundless night pervades me. A black ocean, in which I'm drowning. I'm afraid of never seeing them again, I'm afraid of dying without ever seeing them again. I need a drink. One glass would be enough to dispel my terror. When I feel safe, aggressiveness flares up and flourishes; just now, it's fear. They are far away, they are alone, I want to protect them. I'm so afraid of what might happen to them.

Of course I'm often bored at home, but I feel safe by my wife's side. When I'm not frightened I get bored. When I'm bored, I feel better. Boredom flourishes too, when you feel safe. It's a symptom of security. When I'm angry I feel better still. Anger is courage, it may even become heroism. It's very true that anger is blind. Heroism is unconscious.

I'm going to ring up Paris.

Since the death instinct exists in the heart of everything that lives, since we suffer from trying to repress it, since everything that lives longs for rest, let us unfasten the ties that bind us to life, let us cultivate our death wish, let us develop it, water it like a plant, let it grow unhindered. Suffering and fear are born from the repression of the death wish.

No, no, I want to go on living. To keep on living. I want the company of living men. In a word, I want both to live and to die. To be dead, and yet alive, like everyone else. The great dining-room of this nursing home, white, well kept, well lit, is obviously very wholesome, and the food must be wholesome too, for whatever is not wholesome is not only unwholesome but a lapse from virtue, one's not sure what virtue, perhaps the virtue of being natural: but what is meant by natural or nature is never made clear. These therapists are like mystical-minded boy scouts for whom 'nature' is a religion. And nature, for them, means kitchen gardens, comfortable nature: as if cyclones and earthquakes were not natural.

So then, in this dining-room, at the table next to mine, is a huge, sick old man with a blotchy face; he goes on crutches, he is having rehabilitation treatment. His presence is tolerable. Opposite me is a bald old man with a white beard, a healthy old man, what's known as a fine old fellow: fresh-looking, pink-cheeked, he eats with conviction; he chews his food slowly, his walnuts and hazelnuts, in the way he's been told is good for him. He's quite revolting. He knows, or he believes, that what he eats is giving him life. One mouthful, two hours of life; another mouth-ful, two more hours of life; by the end of the meal he's sure he has won another week of life. But it's chiefly the look in his eyes that is intolerable, the expression of a healthy old man, sharp, cunning and ferocious. I asked to sit at another table; that dogged deter-mination to live, the way he clings to life and won't let go, seems to me tragic, frightening and immoral. I understand it very well, and it's myself that I hate in him, for I cling to life as much as he does, I shall be just like him in a few years' time; I can't forgive him and I can't forgive myself. Why else am I here, if not to get back some zest for life, to eat and grow healthy?

I feel sure that the doctors and nurses in charge of all these fairly affluent people whose sole preoccupation is their will to live, to go on living, must really be somewhat disgusted with them. I don't quite know why, but I find something immoral about this wholesome, virtuous way of eating. I prefer excess, lack of moder-ation, feasting and drunkenness. There's something free and un-fettered about excess: you're not eating to live, you're eating to burst; it's a way of killing yourself.

Z. says to me: 'You say you wanted to learn how to die, but you don't seem really anxious to learn. Here you are with the tense expression of somebody who's not going to surrender, to let himself go. When you've consented to die, you'll be relaxed and calm.'

'I know that,' I said. 'Teach me to unfasten these knots. I know I shall have to unfasten them myself, I know this is a task every-one has got to do for himself, but shed a little light for me so that I can see how these bonds that I cannot undo are fastened.'

'In a sense, you are already dead. You have within you such con-tradictory impulses, inhibiting you, binding you hand and foot, paralysing you, that you're as good as dead.'

'Dead in another sense, since death means surrendering and I cannot surrender. Or else these impulses are killing me in a dif-ferent way. I live like a dead man,' I say quite naturally. Then I burst out laughing as I realize the paradox.

'I was hiding,' said the man, 'this is the beginning of the way.' In the introduction to his book on the Hasidic writings, Martin

Buber reminds us that, according to the Hasidim, the way begins with man's decisive exploration of his heart, but this exploration is only decisive if it really leads to the way, for there is a sort of investigation that is sterile, leading only to self-torture, despair and an even deeper entanglement. This reminds us of the purifying and exorcising function of psychoanalysis, contrasted with the self-analysis of men of letters and writers of journals which is futile and heart-rending.

Every man must find his own way, the Hasidim advise us. The aim of psychoanalysis is not very different; at a certain moment 'light must break'. There are three things to be observed, according to the most ancient teachings, which here converge: 'Know whence you have come, whither you are going and to whom you must render your account.' Alas, I am in pursuit of my soul (anima), which runs far too fast. (The idea that I am already dead pleases and soothes me. This is very superficial. If I were really dead . . . I should know it.)

There are several categories of people: there are those who ask themselves questions, find no answers and resign themselves to not knowing where they have come from or where they are going; there are those who ask themselves no questions, who live content, perhaps because they have unconsciously found the answers; there are those who ask themselves the question and find the answer; finally there are those who ask the question and cannot answer it. I belong to this category. At my age it is too late to hope for an answer. What am I doing here? I understand nothing about it.

I know, I know; I shall be told that my disquiet comes from the fact that I am dissociated from myself. The theoretical explanation is familiar to anyone who has read even a little psychoanalytical writing, particularly Jung's. I suffer through dissociation from the mother-figure, from the feminine principle (anima), from the earth, from death. I therefore project myself on to the non-self, making it into a self, extracting this rapacious self from the non-self which is a more profound self, but which I am unwilling to admit as profoundly myself. Death, this non-self, is my truest, most essential self; this is something one must learn to feel, rather than to understand abstractly. Here, too, there may be a kinship with Oriental thought: is not the non-self which is oneself the 'atman.'

How am I to round this cape, how can I scale the huge wall that figures in my dreams, or bring it tumbling down? How is one to raise the barrier, and who has put me, who has put us in this situation? Just look at men; now they want to live, now they want to die, now they help one another, now they kill each other? No one knows what he wants.

I go round and round in my cage, behind the bars, like a wild animal.

I dream that I am walking in a great park. Around the park there are some white houses, through the windows of which people are staring resentfully at me; at the end of the park there is a small inn. I ask for a drink; the barman replies: 'I can only give you a drink if you show me your certificate of mental health.' 'Why?' I say. 'If everyone had to produce that kind of certificate you wouldn't serve drinks to anyone.' 'Your case is a special one,' the barman replies. 'They say you're a lunatic, you've been having injections, you're under a drug.' I explain that the injections were given me by a doctor, to quell my anxiety; I fail to convince him. I move away. I try to smoke. My cigarettes go out one after the other, they are full of holes that let the air in. I throw them away, one after the other. I go back to the inn, perhaps to buy some more cigarettes. The barman and his shop have both disappeared. There's a cavity in the ground where they were. I kick the spot where the barman had stood, as though to kill him or drive him away symbolically, or to take my revenge on him. At another end of the garden, among the trees, I find a tiny inn. Will they give me a drink here? Three or four people are sitting there, and there's a dark young man who looks at me in quite a friendly way. I go in partly to escape from the hostile stares of the people peering behind the window-curtains in the white houses. I smile to the young man, then I repress my smile. Perhaps I was mistaken; perhaps I only imagined he was looking at me in a friendly way. I was probably wrong. The hostess looks like a good soul, she answers me politely, she's going to give me a drink, she opens a little door which must lead to a back room where they keep the drinks. She agrees to serve me. I sit down at a table and I wait for her to bring me something to eat and drink. But what sort of drink and what sort of food will she bring me? I try to find out, but I cannot. So I wait, I shall soon find out: what's she going to bring me, what's she going to bring me? I wait in vain, I wait and the dream ends with my waiting.

Z. explains (what I know) that this dream contains the elements of an oral obsession. When a child is distressed it is given the breast. Its distress is allayed. Eating and drinking are oral obsessions. It is well known that big eaters and heavy drinkers are often neurotics or near-neurotics. Wanting to eat and drink and being unable to implies separation from the mother-figure that feeds one. To know this is obviously no help to me. In any case, the food I hunger for, the drink for which I thirst are not an infant's food or drink. Knowledge is what I hunger and thirst for. If I really knew what I hunger and thirst for, I should feel easier. As in the dream, I keep on waiting in vain. The tiresome thing about these dreams is that they only show me what I know already. I don't need to dream to discover the reasons for my anguish. I am only too conscious of it. I learn nothing. I don't venture into the unknown. My dreams are too clear. Two small points emerge, however: I must become convinced that the non-self is myself; I must tell myself that I am already dead and that it's not as bad as all that.

I prefer Jung to Freud. Jung does not ban religion. We know that he asserts that it is a psychological need and that since it is a need, it corresponds to a truth. What truth? Is this truth, itself, the symbol of something else, does it conceal something else? That's not what I mean. I dare not: I'm not bold enough to believe.

It was Clémenceau, I think, who said that when a man has character it's usually bad. True; and when one has a conscience, it's usually a bad one. Is it true that Freudian psychoanalysis passes no moral judgment? It seeks to set you free, and that implies passing judgment, since if you are set free it must be from something evil that fetters you. Zen adepts burst into laughter at the sight of a corpse; this implies passing a negative judgment on life, on death, on God. To judge means allotting something a place in a scale of values, it means having a criterion. Zen rejects a manifest God; or else it stands apart from the manifestation, perhaps in order to find a non-manifest God outside it. Zen passes judgment by being 'against' God's manifestation. In any case, to laugh means to combat tears, to struggle against sobs, to be still involved with weeping; even if you overcome those tears, if you laugh you are still passing judgment, you are still moved by passion. In the same way, Freud's concept of man as fettered by anxiety and neurosis implies a judgment. That man is free who does not even know that he is free, nor that there are such things as freedom or imprisonment. The free man is not the man who is beyond good and evil, but the one who is detached from all obsessions with freedom and prison. Wishing to have no more wishes means still having one wish, the wish to have no specific wishes. That man is free, not even free, not even not free, who lives in indifference, neither accepting nor refusing life, for whom to die and to live are the same thing.

To stop thinking, to make one's mind a blank: alas, animals think too, they, too, know fear, they are afraid of death. One cannot not feel hunger and thirst. Why were we created?

I ought to have embarked long ago on this stubborn quest for knowledge and self-knowledge. If I'd set about it in time, I might have achieved something. Instead of writing literature! What a waste of time; I thought I had all of life ahead of me. Now time is pressing, the end is near, and haste is not favourable to my quest; indeed, it's because of literature that I can no longer understand anything at all. It's as though by writing books I had worn out all symbols without getting to the heart of them. They no longer speak to me with living voices. Words have killed images or concealed them. A civilization based on words is a lost civilization. Words create confusion. Words are not speech.

But these words were like masks, or else like dead leaves fallen to the ground. The tree of life and death is still there, bare and black. Nothing now can mask the deepest, most incurable distress. I am face to face with truth.

At Christmas I was in a northern country; here families forgather round a Christmas tree, making merry in their best clothes, and the houses are gaily decked out, people give one another presents, they laugh as if things were going better and better, as if they did not know that the abyss is there. They smile at one another, they are nice and friendly and polite. . . . They exchange kisses as if they adored each other. And yet they are well aware of what is waiting for them. They pretend not to know. How brave they are, how patient they are, how ignorant they are, or perhaps how wise, or perhaps they have some secret, unconscious knowledge of things that I don't know, of all that I cannot succeed in knowing.

I revert to the image of the grey, gloomy, impassable wall of the church. Images are so concise, so profound and complex, and words are so inadequate to translate their living thoughts. Thus, I felt an ardent, urgent need to scale this wall, and I felt at the same time that I could not possibly get over it. Was there a little door down below, on the right? I believe there was, but it was certainly shut. The wall, then, is the wall of a prison, of my prison; it is death, since it looks like a graveyard seen from afar; this wall is a church wall, it separates me from a community; it is therefore the expression of my solitude, of non-interpenetration; I cannot reach others, and they cannot reach me. It is at the same time an obstacle to knowledge, it is what conceals life and truth. In short, what I am trying to pierce is the mystery of life and death, neither more nor less. Naturally such an undertaking seems impossible. But once again my dream only contains my waking thoughts, the image being merely a visual résumé of this impossibility.

It seems to me that when I ponder over this image I discover something which may not be much newer than what I usually think, but is far more precise: why is the earth dark, why is it covered with withered thistles? Because it is a dead land. Why is there no blue in the sky that I can glimpse between the pillars of the cupola on top of the church? Why, after going round the church and passing through the grimy kitchen, did we find ourselves going downhill in those dark, barren fields? Because this is an extinct world, devoid both of fecundity, which is earth's fire, and of celestial light. It is the image of a world, of my world, in which earth is cut off from heaven: a soul, my soul, in which earth is cut off from heaven with all that this means, that's to say myself cut off from myself, my deeper self no longer supplying sustenance to my mind. What's the use of knowing all this when there's still this impenetrable wall separating me, and what is the wall made of? I keep going round in a circle, my problems are still as pressing and as unendurable, and the solution is hidden from me.

At one time I used to have euphoric dreams; dreams in colour; for instance, this one which I had many years ago: I am walking through a green forest, through long grass, light shining through the branches of the trees and at the end of the forest a luminous clearing. Nothing else, save an ineffable joy. If at that time I had been preoccupied with my dreams, if I had tried to probe this dream, or rather to relive it, I might perhaps not have experienced it so fully; but that is what it was, earth and heaven interpenetrating one another, feeding one another and feeding me myself with vital sap. But alas, what that earth may be, what that light may be, that's something I still don't know, or rather something I no longer feel.

The wall also expresses the impassable limit of my being as a man. I don't belong here, I belong elsewhere, and that elsewhere, beyond these walls, is what I have to rediscover; such speculations are quite commonplace. We are all of us obviously limited in our individuality, we are all aware of this. Our finiteness revolts us, or else we realize it and accept it. What is less commonplace is the excessive distress that my limitations cause me: I am not immortal, I cannot know everything, I cannot have infinite knowledge nor be everywhere. If I don't resign myself to this finiteness, if it appears to me as a wall in my nightmares, if it becomes a neurosis, this is no longer something commonplace. Perhaps this is where the harm lies. Since the wall is impassable, I have got to accept it. Not to accept it would be Satanic. In that case the wall must hold. It can only fall down if it cuts me in two. Paradise is perfect adhesion. So there won't be any Paradise. What must we do, then? We must have trust. All priests, wise men, the man in

63

the street tell you so. We must have trust, I tell myself. I tell myself in vain.

R. appears in most of my dreams, in her own shape or else in
some other shape, disguised, as if she didn't want to show herself,
but I unmask her and recognize her. She is there, the perfect interlocutor, myself and another self both at once, sometimes like a
shadow, sometimes reproachful and critical, sometimes my conscience, sometimes a formidable adversary. But she's there; she's
in that withered garden, in that ruined square, she's there, scold-
ing me in front of the church wall she dislikes, she's with me on
that gloomy, barren slope, under that sunless sky. It's clear that
she shares my destiny, whether I want it or no longer want it, or
want it less. It cannot be otherwise, or everything would crumble.
Love or possessiveness? But she does not attempt to lead me, she
goes along with me, simply trying to stop me from losing my
way: from what she thinks is losing my way. The word 'independence' means being lost; if I did not have her with me I
should lose my way. If she were not with me she, too, would
feel lost in misery, astray in a world of chaos, a world whose
foundations had collapsed.

The world, for weeks, seemed no longer the same. A certain
subtle, stealthy alteration. As if the screws of some complex
machine had been slightly loosened, so that it went on functioning
just the same but not quite the same to a careful observer. The
light of the sky had a different tinge, voices and sounds a faintly
altered timbre; a barely noticeable displacement, as if familiar
causes produced familiar effects with difficulty or with some de-
lay. As though there were cracks in the walls of a dwelling
through which an element of strangeness could penetrate. Everything looked and moved and behaved in an altered way, and everywhere there were these imperceptible cracks, that loosened machinery that let in what we know as madness, like a noxious gas
which, once introduced on a large enough scale within the architecture of the universe, might blow the whole thing up.
It is a difficult sensation to define: not the shattering but short-

lived shock that accompanies a sudden vision of unreality, mono-
lithic and undeniable, but the sensation of a beginning of unreality, more insidious, slower and warier, ready to become all-
pervading. The same chaos reigned and yet it was not quite the
same, and yet it was the same. Not the storm of madness, only a
light breeze.

An erotic dream: I am living with a blonde woman whom I
cannot identify. A woman of fashion, since, although naked, she
is wearing white gloves. She goes out with me in this state of un-
dress (but why not stay at home?) and we look everywhere in
the streets, at night, for somewhere to make love, some wall,
some dark corner, some porch. I never succeed in making love,
either through impotence or for lack of time; for we are constantly
interrupted by the appearance of a policeman, and have to go
and take refuge somewhere else. We are short of time for another
reason, too, which is that I have to catch a train and my mistress
has to drive me to the station in her car. We go back to her house,
and I look for my room where I have left my luggage; the stairs
are full of people, and among them I see her husband, who points
to the room where my luggage is waiting: 'Hurry up,' he says
crossly, 'you're going to miss your train!' I hunt for the room,
wandering about the passages; children get entangled in my legs,
I cannot find my belongings. Suddenly the lady reappears, more
fully clothed and wearing a hat. 'Come on,' she says, 'take your
cases or leave them, the train goes in ten minutes.' 'It's too late,'
I say, 'it's too late and I can't go without my cases, I can't leave
them behind.'
  'What do you think of this dream?' Z. asks me. 'How do you
interpret it?'
  The policeman, of course, represents my conscience. I am unable to make love because at the moment I'm in a state of moral
impotence, I can't do what I should like to and, I don't know
how, my moral conscience forbids me to. In any case, you see,
all the dreams I have at present are dreams of failure, of sterility
and prohibition. And yet I want to go, but it's my luggage that
prevents me. I want to take my luggage with me.
  'No,' Z. replies. 'Actually you don't want to be released. The

luggage is an excuse, a pretext. It's the first thing you would give up if you really wanted emancipation.'

The old man who was afraid of death. He used to moan from morning till night about his imminent death. Every time he saw a funeral go by there were tragic scenes: anguish, cries, despair. This went on until the day when, seeing yet another funeral procession pass, one of his nephews had the bright idea of telling him that the deceased was a boy of sixteen. Then every time he asked 'Who has died?' they would answer 'A girl of eighteen', and so forth, until he finally became convinced that only the young die. Funeral processions no longer frightened him; when one went by he would exclaim: 'Another eighteen-year-old has died! The young don't know how to live!'

The libido, or love of life, is not a reassuring love, it is not a free love, it cannot be justified in spiritual terms; only creative love can be thus justified, fatherly love, the love that engenders, that seeks to create living beings. That, indeed, is divine love. Not to want to preserve one's own life but to make others live: to give life if we are not entitled to love ourselves; if it is not right to love ourselves, it is right to love others, not in order to meet one's own reflection in them but because they are truly other than oneself. In this way the world would not be lost.

A few scraps of a dream: a friend of mine, Michel, is dead. He has died in peaceful resignation, and I see him lying there. The remaining images from this dream are hard to interpret: beside him lies his servant, who is his exact double . . . and then this double is transformed into a page of writing from a notebook. I learn that this double, this page of writing, died a week earlier. Michel tells me that he will send me a message presently, bearing the number 139.

Once again I think about the dream in which I saw the great wall: the wailing wall, the wall of separation. I tell myself, all of a sudden, that I ought to make this wall disappear. If I could manage to dream it again, that's what I should try to do. I might try to do this in a state of dream, to concentrate on this mental picture and imagine myself destroying the wall. I have a sort of hope that if I could really succeed in this, something new and unexpected would happen. The sky might brighten perhaps, the withered thistles would bloom again, the barren land would be clothed in green vegetation. In fact I have already tried, during a daytime sleep, to realize this imaginary exploit: I fell into a deep sleep and dreamed about something quite different. A woman was complaining that her husband drank too much and was violent when he had drunk; and in fact he was drinking in the next room, behind a closed door. The woman shows me a half-empty bottle of whisky, the neck of which he had smashed. The door opens and the man appears, a middle-aged man with a small moustache, of medium height and rather thin, but with enormous hands. 'What business is it of yours?' he says to me. I answer him sharply, I scold him and I don't know which of us starts a fight. I realize that he is very strong. I wake up.

I interpret as follows: the man I saw in the dream was one I had noticed a few hours previously and had immediately taken a dislike to. I had seen him in the clinic I go to, a thin middle-aged man with a moustache, just as in the dream. A very powerful voice, too loud for a man of his size. I disliked him because he was telling someone else that all his organs were very sound, that he kept himself fit and did gymnastics in order to have a good time in life and not end up as a decrepit old man. When he talked about his gymnastics I immediately recalled the old Chinese fellow in Hong Kong whom I used to see from my hotel window, doing exercises on his balcony about seven o'clock in the morning before going to work. I had been reminded of an insect, a fly rubbing its wings together among all the other millions of flies. (In fact, why did they have that campaign against flies in China? For hygienic reasons, obviously, but really perhaps because the Chinese are as numerous as flies, to distinguish them from the flies.) This man's powerful hands were not his own hands but those of my masseur. So I think I can see who this man was, with whom I was fighting: it was obviously myself. Almost invincible, as invincible as my self is to myself, that self whom another self tries in vain to overcome.

67

Whatever I may do in this world, disturbing it, transforming it or rather imagining I've transformed it; whatever use I may make of the world, even if I venture into other planets, it is always what it is, and what is that? Nothing can surpass my astonishment at its being what it is, at its being, and at my being there. If I could succeed in opening every door, there would still be the unopenable door of astonishment.

This question, which I know to be insoluble, exhausts me to death. And that, too, is the wall. What does being here mean, what is 'being' and why Being, for ever and ever: why this Being? Suddenly the faint gleam of a crazy hope: the gift of life has been granted us and it cannot be taken away again. I have no clear understanding of what it all means. I don't understand it at all.

Once, when I was an adolescent, and even a little later, astonishment gave rise to euphoria. Let me try once again to describe this state of mind, this happening. I was in a small provincial town and I must have been about eighteen. It was shortly before noon on a luminous day in early June. I was walking about in front of the low white houses of the little town. What happened was quite unexpected. The whole town was suddenly transformed. Everything became at once profoundly real and profoundly unreal. That was exactly what happened: unreality mingled with reality, the two becoming closely and indissolubly interconnected. The houses grew still whiter, utterly clean. There was something quite new and unsullied about the light, this was an unfamiliar world which I seemed to have known from all eternity. A world that the light dissolved and yet reconstituted. An overflowing joy rose up from deep within me, warm and luminous itself, an absolute presence, a presentness. I said to myself that this was 'truth', without knowing how to define this truth. No doubt had I tried to define it it would have vanished. I said to myself, too, that since this experience had happened, since I had lived through it, since I knew everything, although I did not know what it was that I knew, I could never be unhappy again, for I had learnt that man does not die. I should only have to remember these moments to overcome any future distress or anxiety. I had had the essential revealed to me, the rest was inessential. It's true that for some years the recollection of this moment often comforted me. Then it comforted me less and less. Then not at all. When I try to recall that joy I can only see images detached from myself, impenetrable, not quite incomprehensible but impossible to live through again. It's nothing but a cinema film.

Z. tells me that the experience as I describe it to him is quite a characteristic one. It's what is known as a *sartori*, an illumination. He seems surprised that this event should have lost its strength and that the memory of it can do nothing to sustain me. He advises me to try and think of it with concentration.

It was indeed an illumination, that's to say something that takes place in authentic light. Presumably the experience was not a total one. Something was lacking. I thought I had lived through something essential, but the essential part of that essential experience was not in it.

In any case, this euphoria is associated with colours, with plant life, with dazzling light, whether apprehended in a dream or in the waking state. Hence the oneiric images of vegetation and of sunlight filtering through the green branches of trees.

I am constantly relapsing into literature. The fact of having been able to describe these images, of having put them into words more or less satisfactorily, flatters my vanity. I reflect that it may be well written. It may give pleasure to readers or critics. I say this, I tell myself this and then I relapse into literature. The fact of being conscious of it does not save me. The fact of being conscious that I am conscious of literary values only makes things worse. I have to make a choice, though: vanity, the road to failure, or the other thing. One's not always lucky enough to get the knock-out blow, one's not always lucky enough to be desperate about life; I forget it, I seek consolation and amusement, I enjoy myself, I write my 'private diary'. I have tremendous vitality; nothing can exhaust it. Only dreams or nightmares can keep one awake. And yet it seems to me that some of the previous pages had nothing to do with words and writing. If I've relapsed into 'literature', is it because the Administrator of the Comédie Française has just rung me up from Paris to tell me he's interested in my latest play? It doesn't take much to restore my unbalance. Let's eat an apple.

According to the Hasidim, true enthusiasm proceeds neither from mind nor from nature but from the communion of the two. Considering that the Jews have been accused, among other things, of being abstract, of having no feeling for the concrete, people must really have known nothing about them, or not wanted to know anything. More than anyone else, they have a sense of incarnation. One of the Hasidean rabbis condemned, or severely reprimanded, those rabbis or believers whose excessive spirituality kept them too detached from earth, as he also reprimanded those who were too much attached to earth; truth, fullness can spring only from the marriage of heaven and earth. This attitude alone enables us to feel that the manifestation which is life is not futile, that the created world is not to be despised, because it will not be lost. According to this same tradition, earth must rise up to heaven. This is what, in different terms, in terms not so very different, modern psychotherapists tell us when they point out that psychological illness is due to a rupture between the faculties of intuition and sensation. We find the same sense of incarnation in Christian thinkers, notably in Péguy who hopes that whatever has existed will be 'recovered' by eternity. . . . The Hasidim tell the following story: 'Rabbi Dov Baer, the maggid of Mezritch, once begged Heaven to show him a man whose every limb and every fibre was holy. Then they showed him the form of the Baal Shem Tov, and it was all of fire. There was no shred of substance in it. It was nothing but flame. (see Martin Buber, *Tales of the Hasidim*, Thames and Hudson, p. 49.) In Aseniev's book about the Orthodox Church it is said that if a monk laid his hands on the shoulders of a believer or a penitent, or of someone suffering, as we should say today, from anxiety neurosis, the man would feel himself surrounded by a great light. There are the luminous experiences of St John of the Cross, of the Hesychasts, and there are also those of the Neo-Platonists and Plotinus, and of all the mystics. There is Moses' burning bush and Jupiter's fire. Unfortunately it's not enough to talk about them nor to have heard talk of them. If one has not experienced this light, it remains a wretched, futile literary flicker.

This is the question: are we unique beings, that's to say immortal, since that which *is* only once *is* for all time, or are we merely the receptacle for anonymous forces which combine and join within us and then are severed and dispersed? Materialists adopt the second hypothesis; the tiresome thing is that even metaphysical and religious creeds also incline towards it. Only Judaism and Christianity have the audacity to be personalist.

Grow and multiply, religion tells us. At the same time sexual union is not approved of, for it is severely controlled. St Paul even said that men should only marry if abstinence is beyond their power, sex outside marriage being of course out of the question. We must pray for our daily bread, wine is a gift from heaven but we must not drink too much of it, and we must not be greedy. The world is an epiphany, a splendid manifestation of divinity; yet to obtain salvation we must detach ourselves from the world of sense. How can we reconcile this permanent affirmation and this permanent denial of life? Can it be an expression of the incessant struggle between the life instinct and the death instinct? It's hard to strike a balance between the two. Morality, which determines what is to be forbidden, tries to find this balance by means of external restraint. This moral code, this morality, this control of sexuality, of pleasure, of eroticism is the more significant in that it has always been found among Jews as well as among Christians, in bourgeois society and in an even more rigid form in Soviet society, for instance. Revolutionaries reject bourgeois morality, which indeed has no longer any meaning since it is no longer founded on any system of thought, since we no longer know the source or purpose of it; however, through a strange paradox, and under various pretexts which are mere excuses, it has been restored even more firmly in the name of Socialism and is all the more bourgeois because it takes its stand against the moral depravity of the bourgeoisie. . . .

Any way will do. In any case, all the ways are known, they have been analysed and explained: we have them there in front of us, on a tray, like cakes. One can either live for oneself, in freedom, since one man is as good as another and I've as much right as anyone else to take advantage of life; with all the risks this implies, of course, for if one has the right to abandon other people, one finds it hard to accept their abandonment of oneself; or else one can renounce oneself, live only for others, devote one's life to the happiness of others; or else one can be wholly indifferent, expecting nothing from others, expecting nothing from oneself and living in a sort of sage neutrality; or else one can live quite casually, taking what comes and asking oneself no questions of any sort; or else, if one finds existence intolerable, one can commit suicide. All these methods are valid. You only have to choose one of them, a single one, and follow it through to the end. I myself choose them all, but since I cannot follow them all at once I adopt one at a time, only for a couple of minutes of course, then I change my mind and choose another, then I choose the third and so forth. This leaves me in a state of confusion. Fortunately, or unfortunately, I'm a man of letters and I chatter about it all as if I were in a café or a brasserie.

It can't be said that art is devoid of all spiritual value. The artist is, after all, superior to the average man, the technician, the politician, anyone who is wholly unconscious. And yet he doesn't amount to very much. Arthur Rimbaud may have written *Les Illuminations*, people may declare that he was a visionary, but I don't believe in his visions nor in any other literary visions. I don't for one second believe in his illuminations. Art brings a tiny gleam, a tiny greyish gleam, a tiny hint of illumination, swamped in garrulousness.

Of course, words say nothing, if I may express myself thus: at most, an unexpected gesture, an image, an incident, a word come from nobody knows where may propel one into the unutterable experience. Whether I express myself with precision or without, whether my metaphors are apt or inadequate, lost in a flood of confused and rambling verbiage, it doesn't matter; in any case the deepest meaning is lost in explanations. There are no words for the deepest experience. The more I explain myself, the less I understand myself. Of course not everything is beyond the reach of words, but the living truth is. Words only say exactly what can be said, which has been known for a long time. Admitted; and not only admitted but also disputed, considered as inadmissible. But if it's been known for a long time and repeated so often, and we're still no further on, it means that I am right.

A single word can put you on the right track, a second disturbs you, and at the third you panic. With the fourth, utter confusion reigns. The *logos* once meant action as well; it has become paralysis. What's a word? Whatever is not lived with ardent intensity. When I say: is life worth dying for? I am still using words. But at least they're comic. Everyone must have noticed how much talk about language we get from young men from the Sorbonne and the Ecole Normale, from distinguished essayists and journalists, speechifyers and other progressive and wealthy intellectuals. It's become an obsession with them, a mania. If people talk so much about language it's because they're obsessed with what they lack. In the days of the Tower of Babel there must have been a great deal of talk about language too. Almost as much as today. The Word has become verbiage. Everyone has his word to say.

Words no longer demonstrate: they chatter. Words are literary. They are an escape. They stop silence from speaking. They deafen you. Instead of being action, they comfort you as best they can for your inaction. Words wear out thought, they impair it. Silence is golden. It ought to serve as guarantee for speech. Alas, we've got inflation. That, again, is just another word. What a civilization! No sooner do my anxieties withdraw a little than I start talking instead of trying to grasp reality, my reality, the realities, and words cease to be an instrument of search; I know nothing at all; and yet I teach. I've got a word or two to say, too.

Nature saved: herein perhaps lies the superiority of Western religious thought over Oriental philosophies and modern metaphysics. Manifestation is mere appearance, it is nothing, its existence is denied by these Eastern thinkers. For our modern philosophers, manifestation, in other words existence, is everything, there is nothing behind it. For the religious thought of the Mediterranean and European tradition, the Divine spirit is manifest in nature, to which it gives reality: this is Being.

The liberty and generosity of divine love. The world is true, the world 'exists', the world is immortalized.

If you take anxiety to pieces, it vanishes. You dismantle it by elucidating its causes. If you take desire to pieces you abolish desire. This is the aim of Buddhism, as is well known. And this is the unexpressed aim of contemporary psychotherapy.

Z. reminds me that we are not in Paradise and that all we can do is to manage to endure what for some people, including myself, is unendurable. I knew that, we know it. But it's very tiresome. What I want to regain is Paradise. How can one live except in Eden? Any other sort of life is impossible. I like to be settled comfortably and for good.

More about the crisis of language today: actually, no such crisis exists. In a certain sense, that's to say, it does not exist. There's no such thing as the impossibility of communication, except in a single case: between me and myself. Socially, everything is communicable. The assertion that there is no common language is a false statement, conscious of its own falsity. There is propaganda, there are deliberate and sometimes involuntary misinterpretations, but these misunderstandings can easily be cleared up, if everyone makes a sincere effort to define his words and explain his terminology. Men refuse to listen to one another, they refuse to understand one another, they refuse to accept one another; they refuse absolutely. But words are there, clear and precise, to say what there is to be said. We deliberately conceal our thoughts, while revealing them: which is contradictory, but then everything is. At the time of Molière, who was not a fool nor a second-rate mind endowed only with common sense, as is sometimes said today, pedantry and preciosity warped understanding. The *précieux* deliberately sought to create an incomprehensible language, they wanted to segregate themselves from other people. Today, there is deliberate segregation. People refuse to understand, they refuse to let themselves be understood except by their own faction. Besides, I don't think anyone believes in this crisis of language any longer. The existing systems of expression, that's to say the few philosophies or ideologies that are still in force, have been seen through. What there is to be said can be said. What needs to be said, that which is existence and not just a thing, this alone refuses to be said. The essential. In short, we need only to purge our language of ideological pedantry and propaganda, that's to say of a certain terminology that deliberately falsifies exact reality (and this can be seen both in the Press reports of world affairs and in those articles and studies that 'analyse' facts and 'situate' them in their strategic or tactical context) and from the trickery of politicians. Everything can be said clearly if it is conceived clearly, if nobody hinders you and conceals the truth from you. The only thing that remains to be expressed is the truth, which is inexpressible. We can't do it. But what those who talk of the crisis of language and the impossibility of communication describe as incommunicable is perfectly communicable.

A. is an idiot, a bastard, a swine! You can say of anybody that he is an idiot, a bastard and a swine. You can say it of everyone and of no one. Underlying every vice, all lust, in the heart of every murderer, behind what appears to us as jealousy, treachery or cowardice, sometimes even more than at the base of every virtue and every loyalty, there is a questing aspiration towards the absolute, there is a nameless yearning.

They are like birds, stupid, insensitive, ferocious. A universe of ferocious birds. That's what I seem like myself to others, that's what I am for them. Sometimes the hidden monstrousness breaks out, reveals itself, our monstrous hellish abysses are disclosed. Vain efforts have been made to exorcise and uncover the secret springs of hatred. How can we rid ourselves of this hell? I terrify myself, and every new face makes me panic; what hell, what sort of hell is hidden behind this façade?

We know others primarily under their polite, reserved aspect. We must venture no further, we should fall into the abyss. Whom have you killed, at any rate in your heart, you there dressed in your Sunday best? And you, pretty lady, how many people have you wanted to kill, whom do you still want to kill, would you like to accept my services to rid you of those who are in your way? . . . Since the world is no Paradise, it can only be a Hell, unless we abolish all desires. Where there is desire there is frustration of that desire, lack of satisfaction, hell. Is there anyone who does not long for everything, even if he's not aware of it? The world does not belong to me, nothing and nobody belong to me; who is wise enough to admit this honestly? Who will accept the fact that he possesses nothing? Imagine champion runners politely inviting one another, at the start of the race: 'After you, sir, please go first.' 'Not at all, after you. . . .'

But the ostensible goal of the race is not its true goal. The man who wants to get there first (and who doesn't?) is a swine. Of course. But the true goal, concealed from us by the apparent goal, the thing we desire over and above desire and despite desire justifies us, redeems us, not morally (for what is morality?), and because this goal bears witness that we have gone beyond our own limits, that we are limitless.

Living is so painful. Longing so keenly to live is a neurosis; I cling to my neurosis, I have got used to it, I love my neurosis. I don't want to be cured of it. That's why I get these terrors, that panic at nightfall.

Old men long to kill. Old men are vile. The young are second-rate and stupid. I always detested the young, particularly when I was young myself. The way our intellectual leaders, in search of disciples, pay court to youth is one of the most depressing things I know. It's so undignified, so contemptible, so absurd!

We have the past behind us, the future before us. We don't see the future, we see the past. That's odd, for we haven't eyes in the back of our heads.

I am alive. It's warm in this room. The light is shining. I take up a book. When I'm too frightened I take shelter in the moment: a precarious nest.

The young are aggressive, the old cling. It takes as much energy to be aggressive as to cling; or perhaps clinging takes more.

I am lying down, but not asleep, and my imagination is active; I see, once more, the wall I had dreamed about. Good. It symbolizes among other things my separation from myself. It is also what separates me from the truth or from a more accurate and more extensive knowledge. I have to find out what lies behind it. On the right, there's the little closed door. I go up to it, and look through the keyhole; I see an eye watching me. I retreat. Then I go up again and look through the keyhole once more. A spurt of water hits me in the face and in the eyes. I retreat. Then I go back for a third look. I barely have time to move aside: someone shoots an arrow through the hole and it flies past me and disappears in the darkness of one of the ruined houses behind me, looking like a decayed tooth. A second black arrow, then a third, then a fourth are shot out through the same hole. I move away from the door and go back to stand in front of the wall in the arid garden. This time R. is on my left; to my right other arrows brush past me threateningly. I know they won't hit me but they warn me not to go near the door. Suppose I make a frontal attack on the wall? I rush at it and to my surprise make a largish hole. I look through it. I see nothing but blackness, chaos. I stare into the blackness; amid the dense gloom I can make out tiny whitish things, which I take to be germs. I go through the breach I've made in the wall, in spite of a certain anxiety, and find myself alone in the darkness. I get used to it. I see a well at the bottom of which is a faint grey light. I go down the well. I reach the bottom, and find myself in one of the bath- and massage-rooms at my clinic. As usual after a bath, I am lying stretched out on the leather couch, covered with towels and wrapped up in blankets like a mummy. In this room it is daylight. The well opens up above me. I feel as if I were in a crypt. Lying thus, I must look like the recumbent statue on a tombstone, such as one sees in cathedral crypts. Then the blankets that cover me are removed, I get dressed and climb up the well, where an iron ladder now stands against the wall. I see myself reaching the first floor of the clinic, then the second floor, by the staircase, I go into Z.'s room and ask him: what am I to do?

I imagine myself going back in front of the church. I manage to block up the hole again. The place where I had made the hole is visible as a whiter patch on the wall, with fresh stones and plaster.

I stop thinking about the wall.

From time to time, a certain euphoria. What is it due to? To my solitude, to the strict diet and the medical treatment which have enabled my organism to get rid of its toxins? To the fact that I am getting rid of my toxins by writing about them, that's to say projecting them outside myself? Is it simply the drug 'isidon', which I have been taking for the past ten days and which must be beginning to take effect? And yet all last night, as yesterday evening and again this morning, I was down that hole, in distress. They say it's the vicious wind from Zürich that causes these depressions; there must be euphoric winds too. It's not philosophy that can cure us or make us ill; we are at the mercy of the wind.

We are all afraid of having made a failure of our lives. There's a certain bogus philosopher, unattractive in appearance and in personality, who has contributed nothing to philosophy, but has merely tried to reconcile existentialism and Marxism, and who, since he lives in a country that permits opposition, has been able to be in opposition without any risk to himself, in perfect freedom, and whose opposition is not even authentic, since it merely conforms to current tendencies expressing the petty bourgeoisie's jealousy of the big bourgeoisie, with the full connivance of the bourgeois authorities which, after all, are flattered by the expression of such resentment; this great philosopher who, by displaying his resentment, has acquired world-wide fame, wealth and esteem instead of the contempt he deserves, tells us sadly in one of his books that his life has been a failure.

But there's another man, who spent twenty years of his life in prison for political reasons, and lived for seven of those years in solitary confinement, and who has just emerged from prison; he does not complain of a wasted life. He is sixty-two, in good health, rejuvenated; he feels that his life has been a full one and that moreover it's beginning again. He was not allowed to read or write, which enabled him to develop his memory to a considerable extent. Being a mathematician, he made certain mathematical discoveries under these stringent conditions.

When he came out of prison he telephoned his friends and relations, and learned that his mother, his sister and brother-in-law had died in the meantime. Most of his friends, some of whom had become ministers or writers of repute, in favour with the government of the country, were also dead. Many of them, before dying, maintained that they had made a failure of their lives. But nothing could impair the delight of the liberated prisoner, who immediately began reading mathematical books and journals to find out whether his own discoveries coincided with contemporary mathematical researches.

Another man, a musicologist, after fifteen years in prison, including several in solitary confinement, was full of confidence on his release; he is now writing down the music that he composed in his head while in prison. He lives in a small village in the plain. He hates nobody, he bears nobody a grudge, he does not complain of having wasted his life. He's said to be a sort of saint. Reclusion has its advantages. It has long been known that asceticism purifies the soul by giving it calm and wisdom. There is a third man, too, who was arrested and condemned to several months' imprisonment for having been caught reading the French paper *Le Monde* in a totalitarian country. He served his sentence; meanwhile, the course of events brought about the liberalization of his country and the power of the oppressors was considerably reduced. What did the man see, a few minutes after leaving prison? A newspaper stall displaying, among other papers, *Le Monde*, which anybody could now buy openly. 'I ought to have waited,' the man thought, 'that's what comes of wanting the latest news!' A reflection made without bitterness towards anyone, himself included. It was just his lot.

But those people who are at liberty, and who think themselves free because they are at liberty, are sour or embittered, resentful or jealous, dissatisfied or pessimistic. Probably because they have not fully served their sentence.

My only justification for speaking of myself is that I am sufficiently detached to discuss myself as though I were somebody else, a case liable to interest psychologists and so forth. One says that; I wonder if such self-justification is not hypocritical; but then again every case, even my own, is interesting. Anybody's universe, every living creature's, an ant's, can be fascinating. Everyone's universe is universal.

79

I put too much faith in the myth of psychoanalysis. It contains a truth, but I exaggerate its truth, since I probably don't know enough about psychoanalysis. I have not yet acquired a critical attitude towards it. Even if I wanted to, I could not have one for the time being. In one sense, a myth is an exaggeration, an amplification, a generalization, an 'absolutization' of a certain truth, of a truth that is certain. When I exaggerate the truth of psychoanalysis, for instance, I make of it, involuntarily, a sort of supreme science which encroaches on other fields, on other truths that conflict with it.

I find myself on the top of a hill. Below me lies a wood or a dense thicket. There's a lot of grass, but it's grey, like the wood and the sky; yet there is vegetation, the grass is thick and probably damp. (Z. tells me the vegetation is a good sign.) A little railway station on this hill or mountain-top. A train with uncovered trucks. I take the train; I see no other travellers. I lie down in one of the open trucks, and the train moves slowly down the hill. At the bottom, at the end of the rails which are gleaming because it must have been raining, I catch sight of a dark tunnel. I feel a certain anxiety. We move forward, reach the bottom of the hill, close to the mouth of the tunnel; the engine goes in, the trucks follow, and mine in its turn, still uncovered, moves into the dark passage. My anxiety increases slightly. Then, once I am inside the tunnel, it disappears. The darkness is all around me; no opening to right or left, nor overhead; a dark, semi-circular ceiling. It is strange that my anxiety should have utterly vanished; not only do I feel no fear, but on the contrary I am filled with a sense of well-being. I am there in the darkness while the train moves gently forward, I feel relaxed, happy, sheltered, totally secure. We emerge from the tunnel: a grey light, a little building like a strange station, dark vegetation. I wake up.

I had had to consent to travel down the slope, to lie down and relax. I had had to conquer my anxiety. Once anxiety was conquered, there was the warm, humid tunnel that meant security, the peaceful tomb, surrender, solitude, that's to say separation from people, from the world, from life. I don't understand why I came out of the tunnel again. In any case I woke up happy, as if

I were freed from a baseless anxiety, from irrational fears. My happiness lasted for a full half hour after my awakening.

We are in the street together, she and I, in a town that reminds me of Paris, of Zürich, and, somewhat, of that part of Athens that lies at the foot of the Acropolis. It is also rather like that wholly imaginary town, always the same, through which I some-times wander in my dreams. I tell her that we shall soon reach the tramway station close to the river, which is partly the Seine, partly the lake of Zürich, and partly some other watercourse. We take the tram, which brings us gradually to the upper town, up in the mountains. The tramway is at the same time a sort of cable car line. I recognize the district, or the town, with its houses perched high up on the mountain side, and it makes me feel euphoric because of its height. The tram, or train, or cable car, passes over narrow ridges where there's only room for the rails. We cross over a narrow footbridge, we climb up mountains where the trees grow among the houses. Then we go down again and find ourselves once more in the lower town. We decide to have dinner at home, in the small hotel where we live in a student's bed-sitting-room. We go out to buy bread, and I go into a baker's and take half a loaf, which I give her. Then I tell her I have just met some friends and on the spur of the moment invited them to dinner with us. She's annoyed, and scolds me for having issued such a casual invitation. 'We haven't enough bread,' she says, 'and the bakers' shops will all be shut.' The argument grows heated; I try to reassure her, I tell her to go home, that I'll get the bread myself. I take her as far as the lift, and then she's inside the cage and we are accusing one another violently. How can we go on living together after what we've said to each other? one or other of us says. She disappears. I am seized with remorse, I go in search of her, terrified of not finding her; I go into another house where, for some reason, I'm convinced she must be. At the door a concierge says: 'Don't go in, they're supposed to be having a cocktail party, but it's really a trap laid by the Germans, who have got all these people together so as to make a raid and pick out hostages. You and she are both on the list. Don't go in, run away.' Whatever happens I can't leave her trapped there alone. I feel I've got to see her at all costs. I go inside, I look for her, I discover her among the crowd; the Germans are already there. I take her by the arm, and while the Germans go round scrutinizing people and arresting them, I manage to get out by a secret door, still holding her by the arm. We are out in the street behind the house with two or three other people who have escaped too. She is sitting on the pavement; then she's in an uncovered railway truck. Is the train going to start? If it gets off before the Germans arrive in search of us, we are saved. 'I don't care whether they find us or not, whether they let us go or shoot us,' she tells me. 'Whether I live or die, I don't care, I love you, you love me,' she adds, flinging her arms round me. So I shall have known love; love is the strongest thing of all. I have given everything, I have achieved everything, I shall have known love. Once you have had that experience, it makes no difference whether you live or die. I am happy, for at last I know the truth, I know the answer. Slowly the train moves off, taking us away; we can still see the house, then we can no longer see it. We are out of danger. I wake up. A great happiness, which lasts for a quarter of an hour, until the moment when I am completely restored to the waking world, to everyday life. It can't be true, I think, and my happiness fades.

If there were no death! Nobody would hate anyone else. Nobody would be jealous of anyone. We should love each other. We could begin everything over again, indefinitely, and from time to time something would be achieved; once in a hundred or a thousand times the chances are we'd be successful. We know that we haven't the time to go on taking risks indefinitely. Hatred is the expression of our anxiety, our lack of time. Jealousy is the expression of our fear of being abandoned: abandoned in this mortal life, abandoned in life, abandoned in death. How can we finish the journey, except hand in hand? And even so! We're always told that every living creature needs affection, that one cannot live without affection, that the great misfortune is to feel unloved. Every psychologist knows that. Love is the air we breathe, our daily bread. But alas, the air is polluted and the bread poisoned.

Which is the right way? Indifference, perhaps. That's not possible; since we are here, we can't help participating; we can't be detached from the manifest world, since we are immersed in it. Let's assume, then, that everything is comic; let's laugh at it. That would be an insult to God or to the world. We cannot soar above it all, we cannot be superior to the Divinity, we cannot be more powerful than the Creator. That's a piece of folly. Let's have a sense of humour. We cannot reject the world. Then let's take everything seriously; that's equally ridiculous. Earnestness is fatal; being earnest means taking sides, falsifying issues. Shall we just let ourselves live? But we shan't be allowed to. Suicide is unforgivable failure; and we must not fail. To say that the world is absurd is equally ridiculous; we're not more intelligent than the Deity. It is absurd to say that the world is absurd. What criteria have we for absurdity? If I say that history is absurd, I imply that I know something which is not; therefore the absurd no longer exists. Am I to commit myself? That means siding with a part against the whole, it means being on the wrong track, going astray. Shall I accept existence as it is? If I say what it is I am still passing judgment, and I cannot fail to be mistaken since my intelligence is limited. I can confine myself to the details of living, to particular truths and actions: in that case I am dissociated from myself, broken up, alienated. Or I can be like a tree: but I'm not a tree. Or I can follow the drift of history, in the direction of cosmic evolution. Nobody knows quite what that means. I can make assumptions, but then I am not making a conscious choice. Pascal's wager: in order to wager one ought to know what one is wagering for, and against whom or what. I don't know the basic elements of the game. One ought at least to feel at ease; I cannot, because living is the source of my unease, because living means living anxiously. I cannot even say that, since, not knowing what the sources of my anxiety are, I don't know what it is that I call anxiety. Anxiety is ignorance. Non-anxiety is also ignorance. I cannot say that I know nothing, for I don't know what knowing means and I don't know what the expression 'means' means. I seem to be going round in a circle. Perhaps I'm not going round in a circle. Perhaps there is no circle. I cannot laugh, nor weep, nor sit down, nor lie down, nor get up, nor desire, nor not desire, for what does one desire or not desire? I am paralysed. I cannot move. But I do move. It seems to me, it seems to me.

It seems to me, too, it seems that someone, some sort of supreme consciousness must be laughing heartily at us. Perhaps this consciousness is not laughing, it seems to me that it doesn't seem to be, it doesn't seem to me that it seems to.

The Fiery Coconut Palm

Disheartened, dismantled, disintegrated. You can see why: the clattering factories, mechanical cats, automated calvaries, factitious metamorphoses, the monocular earth, the sound and fury of great cities, electricity, astronautics: the modern world. I'm running away, to rediscover my homeland, the land of olive trees.

Air. Sea. Huts, streams, leaves, lanes, round and round. Giant foliage. Was this Jamaica? Oh, surely not! Surely yes: the broad spaces, the narrow places, the lily chariots, pure nature with its Gioconda smile, the beautiful boat in the beautiful blue sea, the white boat among all those red rocks, the white boat among all those green meadows. The weeping willows danced and drowned their locks in the cool rivers of four dawns! The breeze whipped up by the young rising sun: its forest-coloured tunic, warmed by the sun. Echoes multiplied, reverberated the thousand shattered fragments of light. Sun-castles of which the sun was only the shadow. Living fireworks. My amazement.

Then the Calm stretched out its long lazy length, covering us. Cool blue snow from four quarters. At night, caressed by the Calm, hearts quiver, hearts sigh, hearts cease sighing, cease quivering, tangible hearts! We are at last what we are; what d'you think of that?

Unexpectedly the mute spoke: 'We're on the Pacific shore, don't be too sure, the Pacific's tricky.' When I stared back, bewildered: 'Yes, yes, it's a wicked trickster.' He moved away, leaving his eyes behind him.

Shoulder-shrugging, I thought: 'There's more to it than that.' Then I lay down comfortably purring, pulling the coverlet over me.

Buried for hours, numb with splendour, my head had long been sunk in Sunday velvet.

Suddenly, suddenly, suddenly, suddenly, suddenly the front gate clanged. I saw myself amid the debris: flaunting immense red curtains, an extraordinary Saint-Sulpice! The sky poured lakes into the oceans. The Universe! I stared at its thousand periwigs, sparkling millions, fabulous nebulae. It utterly overturned orientation; and on a stage bounded by no banks, there rose up—joyful, merry, all arteries out-

spread, all delights blossoming, all balloons flying, the virgin forest around it welcoming it with merrymaking—there rose up, fierily glowing, there arose and spread out, covering us from eyes to feet, from toes to neck, from brow to belly, all fire, all flame, the greatest of all: the coconut palm, the baobab!

Back from my holidays I tried to tell them. A well-known phenomenon, they said: a commonplace affair. A tall story!

Vinea, one of the greatest of his country's poets, translated my play *The King Dies*. I had known him once, very long ago. I remember him as a great gentleman. He was a handsome man, he spoke little, he was sensitive, intelligent, and not a fascist like most of the 'intellectuals' of his country. When the extreme left took power he stood aside. This was a sane and honest reaction. He did not want to have his mind shackled, he did not want to be bought. He was a free man who loved freedom for others: he did not take advantage of tyranny, he endured it with resignation, although each successive régime sought his complicity. Neither master nor servant. A solitary aristocrat. In the course of events, after having kept him in the background, those in power reviewed his position, as the phrase is. They admitted that he was a great poet, they published his works; such nobility, such integrity and intransigence had ended by impressing openly those who had already been impressed without daring to say so, as well as the rest who decided, one fine day, that this was a good moment to display admiration for a man whose moral courage had never failed. But physically his strength was declining and now, at the age of seventy, he has just died.

I was happy to learn that it was he who was translating my play, proud that he had chosen to do so, and deeply distressed to learn at the same time that he was on the point of death, that he was dead. I had felt the radiance of his personality but I had never really got close to him. In any case, one cannot get to know anyone through conversation, nor even by taking his hand, nor even by walking close beside him. It is only through another's writing, that's to say his confession, it's only by immersing oneself in his universe, in his innermost depths, that communion can be achieved. Here, after all, is a justification of literature. This postulate is no longer a commonplace, for if it is often asserted it is seldom realized. Alone with another man's work, alone with that other man, who is not even aware of your experience, of your approach to him, who does not know that you have come to know him truly and profoundly; the other man's world becomes your world. The intimacy is profound, discreet and total.

Vinea died just as he had finished the translation. What can it have meant to him, can it have brought him any help? I had written the work so that I might learn to die. It was to be a lesson, a sort of spiritual exercise, a gradual progress, stage by stage, towards the ineluctable end, which I tried to make accessible to other people. When my play was put on in Paris and abroad a certain number of critics alleged that it contained only commonplace thoughts, ideas already known or foreseeable; perhaps it was because these people, these spectators, thought themselves merely at a play and were unwilling to live through an adventure which in one sense must be commonplace, of course, since it belongs to us all, but which is fundamental if one tries to experience it fully. Can this text have helped Vinea to die? It didn't help me in the least; as I wrote it, I seemed to be rejecting my own words. It became just one more play, and I became just another spectator, somewhat more sensitive than the rest but, all the same, detached from myself. If I only knew whether it had brought him anything, and what it may have brought him! If it helped anyone to feel less anguished, to accept his fate, I should feel joy, relief, a sense of justification. If there is a chance that it taught others, something, that would perhaps encourage me to think that I might be able to profit by my own teaching.

They say that pity for others is really only a form of self-pity. Is such pity monstrous, because it is only pity for myself? Everything, we know, is just a projection of oneself. It is surely better, though, to project one's pity on to others than to keep it for oneself. I realize that I need love in order to live. I conclude that others, in order to live, need love. Perhaps self-pity leads to self-disgust, to self-hatred. If one is too sorry for oneself one can't endure oneself any longer. Of course one has to love oneself; if one does not love oneself one hates others too. This projection is well known, too. One must keep a little love aside for oneself and give the rest to others. One can't give it all; one would die of inanition. My rationed generosity justifies my own existence. The feeling of guilt is due, paradoxically, to the fact that I am giving too much, as well as to the fact that I am not giving enough. The man who gives everything becomes like someone dying of hunger and thirst, lying on the ground, pale, gasping, begging for a glass of water. It's going to be an endless business feeding him. The man who has given everything takes everything back. He is insatiable. You'll have to feed him with your own blood. The man who has given everything becomes a vampire.

I am torn between regret and remorse. But one has to make up one's mind, one has to choose between regret and remorse. One can't endure them both at once. Remorse: I feel guilty of having wronged others. Regret: I feel guilty of having wronged myself. I exchange regret for remorse, then remorse for regret. This is real constraint, real imprisonment. In the morning, regret; as soon as night falls, here comes remorse. Regret looks like selfishness; have I the right to be selfish? Can I choose between what harms me least, can I choose between myself and the other person as I would between two objects, when we are both living beings, existences? Regret is hard to endure, but it is clear-cut, it remains concrete. Remorse first assumes another person's face, then that face fades away, is swallowed up in darkness, and remorse becomes a faceless anguish.

I demand the right to settle matters with myself. To be face to face with myself. Perhaps from my confrontation with myself something else may emerge. 'Don't change, don't let all this anxiety rise to the surface, close your eyes, you wouldn't be able to endure it.' But in any case I can't endure myself, it's time for me to become aware of things. It's time to assert myself. What's the good of struggling, says the other voice, what's the good? But I'm crippled, I'm choking, I'm dying because I cannot die, I cannot know. If I could only consider myself as already dead, my anguish would have died too. Consider myself as dead? I shan't succeed in doing that until death has killed me. I know, I know, it's better to kill oneself than to let oneself be killed. It seems to me an inaccessible mountain peak. And since I think it's impossible, it's no use my thinking of it any longer, it's nothing but literature. The world of literature, the impotent world, the world of partial lucidity, between strength and weakness. We should seek action, which means forgetfulness; or supreme lucidity, which is religion. There is no escape through literature; action, at least, provides that. I lament my impotence, I know what my sickness is, I describe it; I cannot reach its deepest source. As soon as I say to myself that these pages may perhaps be published, their truth is corrupted. They become counterfeit coins. Such introspection is valueless, sterile, harmful. It is not the knowledge that leads to the right path, the path that brings one out into the light.

Yes, I claim the right to settle matters with myself. The right to be alone, face to face with myself. You're forgetting us, others say, you cannot desert us. But if I become strong, if I am set free, I will give you some of my strength, my freedom. They know my failings, they know the precise location of my weak points. That's where they thrust in knives . . . or make pinpricks, tiny pinpricks.

I should like to spend my whole life in a nursing-home, in a bright bare room in a nursing-home. Since we're in prison, I'd as soon have this sort of prison. Particularly, of course, if it's a prison where they allow you to go out once or twice a week. Prison means shelter. I get on quite well with solitude, or rather I'm learning to get on better. I can stay alone in my room from six o'clock in the evening without getting bored. I write, I read, I do crosswords or I do nothing at all. My anxiety has not disappeared, but I can bear it better than I used to. If only I could be allowed to stay here. Not so long ago, if I happened to be alone I'd have done anything to find someone with whom I could pretend to talk. Now I shut myself up, I settle down into my fear, I wrap it over me, I sink into it as into a bed.

While I am concentrating on my own problems, while I am struggling with myself, a great many men are living in misery or killing one another, making war on each other; 99 per cent of those who are fighting don't want to do so; like me, they are prisoners; but not of themselves, of their leaders, who alone can choose what to do or not to do, can decide for or against, and order the slaughter. A whole country is up in arms, so the formula runs, ready to die for its independence, a whole nation seeks to free itself from its oppressors, united, so they say, in hatred for American imperialism, capitalist exploitation or some other exploiter or tyrant. These are crude, twopence-coloured pictures, or cruel irony: the Algerians were so anxious to get rid of the French colonists that as soon as the Algerian war was over, shiploads of them were brought back to France to find work and a little bread. In the district where I was then living, I saw a fine American car in which four well-dressed Arabs were travelling, with a woman, a sort of Pasionaria. The car stopped every twenty or thirty yards, at one Arab shop after another, to collect goodwill contributions towards the ultimate goal. There was no sign of goodwill on the face of the shopkeeper who had been collected from. And there was no goodwill about that poorly-dressed Arab who lay dying on his doorstep, who had surely not been executed on account of his excessive goodwill and his keenness to fight. In certain East European countries there is such hostility to American capitalist exploitation that twenty years after the liberating revolution these countries are glad to welcome back American firms with American capital. Wretched indeed was the lot of those Danubian peasants who walked barefoot along the roads, but carried their shoes on their backs because their feet were too hot, and who had nothing to eat but bread, bacon, eggs, white cheese, onions, potatoes and now and then a small chicken whose neck had been wrung in the poultry-yard where dozens of other birds were awaiting the same fate. These unfortunate peasants were in difficulties, because compulsory education had already been introduced and they could not keep their children at home, so there was nobody but the poor peasant woman to milk the cow. But that's not the point, and I seem to be getting involved in politics; what I mean is this: men who are in prison obviously want freedom, those who are hungry want something to eat, and a man who is fighting in a war is afraid of war, he is afraid and he overcomes dangers, he is afraid of dying here and now; he is happy, when the fighting ends, to have escaped death, and he has unlimited time, almost an eternity, to live before to-morrow comes. Fear of danger drives out anxiety. Anxiety is the feeling of being surrounded by countless invisible dangers, dangers that have no concrete form, that are faceless. It is so natural to live in need and danger, that anxiety takes the form of distress at being deprived of that familiar, indispensable danger which is concrete, real and visible, which can be attacked and against which one can defend oneself. Anxiety is the danger that lurks in darkness. You can't believe in the absence of danger; it seems to be a treacherous snare. The enemy against whom I have to fight or from whom I must escape is no longer a man or a tiger but a whole army of invisible and intangible monsters. Danger means life; anxiety is deadly. It is the fear of unknown dangers. I am threatened, but by what, by whom, which way am I to face? I hit out blindly into the void. Danger is the fear of dying, of being killed. Anxiety is the fear of death itself.

The greatest crime of all is homicide. Cain kills Abel. That's the crime *par excellence*. And we keep on killing. I have to kill my obvious enemy, the one who is trying to put me to death, in order that he shall not kill me. In killing him I find relief, for I am obscurely aware that I have killed Death. I am not responsible for his death, I can feel no anxiety on that account, if I have killed my adversary with the approval of the community; that's what wars are for, to enable one to kill with a clear conscience. By killing I exorcise my own death; the act of killing is part of a magic rite. When the Germans killed the Jews they did so with a clear con-science, for they 'killed in self-defence'. Weren't the Jews going to exterminate or conquer the entire world? Weren't they cor-rupting the health and morals of the Aryan race, which is another form of murder? Sustained by an ideology derived from the *Genesis of the Nineteenth Century* by the Englishman Houston Chamberlain, from the Comte de Gobineau and the more rudi-mentary French racialists of the nineteenth century, using further-more the more recent and concrete examples of Russian pogroms (pogrom is a Russian word, a Russian action) and the Soviet death-camps, adding to this their own cruelty, the Germans felt them-selves justified. Anti-semitism is not of German origin; it is Russian,

Polish, French. I won't go so far as to say that the Germans were simple-minded sheep gone mad, but they had antecedents from elsewhere. The Germans felt themselves guilty only when a vaster community denounced and condemned them. Permission to kill had lost its mystique; they no longer had the approval of everyone else. At that moment the whole German nation felt like a single individual condemned by society, indicted by an assembly of all the nations. It is true that their explosion of hatred for humanity was something authentically and objectively guilty. I feel a horror mingled with a sort of admiration for those who assume the responsibility of killing all by themselves, of deciding to live a murderer's life, the freeshooters of death, such as professional gunmen. What courage, what defiant strength; such people have no super-ego. We know now that existence means aggression. We know, too, that society is divided, that the different social categories war on one another. That each social category has a clear conscience, since it is a collective unit. In an absolute sense, no social category has more reason to have a clear or a guilty conscience than any other. To destroy the clear conscience of a social category and strengthen that of one's own category is the aim of propaganda. Taine, more perspicacious and deeper than Karl Marx, had already shown that the aristocracy succumbed because it had become aware that it had lost its usefulness. The nobles abdicated (the night of August 4th, etc.). The collapse of a class is only possible when that class gives up the struggle. Of course it may subsequently regret its abdication, and realize that others have no better reasons than itself for . . . etc. David Rousset has shown us that a concentration camp is a society like all existing societies, like all social organizations; a concentration camp is society in its essence, in its quintessence. Kafka, again, described the concentration camps before they existed. He knew.

Kafka, like Christ, took the guilt of the world upon him. That is his sense of guilt. Of what are we guilty? Of a crime against love. And Sigmund Freud, that other great Jew, that great rabbi, in the purest tradition of the rabbis, doctors of the soul, sought to exorcize hatred. The Jews invented love, the love of others, fatherly love, divine love. That's the reason why they have been accused of hatred.

To imagine one's own death is impossible. And we have to try, just because it's impossible.

Here's a rope; it is knotted. I untie the knot. No more knot, what has become of it? The rope remains. Other knots can be tied with the same rope. I am a knot, I am the rope; am I the knot rather than the rope?

Freud, knowing what he felt the need of—love—knew what others needed. He realized, too, that we must not repress aggressiveness. Life must be made into loving aggressiveness; aggression sweetened by love. Thus one can be killed in an easier fashion, die a very easy death: a ritual death.

H. is divorcing his wife. She is brave and unhappy, the children are unhappy too. H. has an uneasy conscience, feels guilty, etc. He is horribly unhappy. His new wife wears a tragic look, she's developing an enormous sense of guilt too. Each one of them takes for granted an unhappiness which they've deliberately sought.

H. tells me that a psychotherapist friend of his has been taken up with two difficult cases, two people who don't know each other and who have been coming to see him every day for the past two or three months: a man and a woman. The man would like to be divorced, but inwardly he cannot face divorce, so he never achieves it. The psychotherapist tries to explain to him the reasons for his behaviour, he does his best to help the poor man to separate from his wife.

The other patient, the woman, is suffering from nervous depression because her husband wants to leave her. The psychotherapist tries to explain to her that to keep her husband she must behave in a different way. He tries to make her admit that it is largely her own fault if her husband wants to leave her. Every morning at nine o'clock the psychotherapist sees the man whom he is trying to help get a divorce; at ten, he sees the woman whose husband he wants to prevent from divorcing her. One day, if the doctor were feeling tired, he might make a mistake and confuse the treatments.

Hans could not accept the way that his wife always put herself in the right, and accused him of being alone to blame for their misunderstandings. She did not for a moment doubt the rightness of her own case, her absolute innocence. He was entirely in the wrong, whereas she was always being wronged. As she never did wrong and he never did right, he would have to admit, if peace were to be restored after their domestic scenes, that he alone was in the wrong. He would have to capitulate. She demanded total, unconditional capitulation. Naturally, since she was right. She always managed to put him in the dock. He protested, of course, with all his might, he tried to justify himself, to explain himself, to find excuses for himself. And so the more he protested, the deeper he got bogged down in guilt in his wife's eyes, and perhaps even in his own. Any discussion was in vain, he always came up against a blank wall, a deaf wall, for she was deafness incarnate; of course he threw fits of fury, and that was just what she was hoping for, consciously or not. In this way, when she had made him really angry, he was bound to feel a sense of guilt and an overwhelming remorse; and so he capitulated after every argument, every day, several times a day, for years. In the end she always forgave him. No agreement, no bargaining, no settlement, no understanding; it was no small thing to have been granted his pardon.

All of a sudden, lightheartedness and joy. For years and years I had not felt like this. Everything had seemed wearisome, tedious, drab and dreary; I had been incapable of reading a book, taking an interest in any conversation, any entertainment. I used to avert my eyes. Everything was a burden, an imposition: writing plays, watching plays, parties, professional or merely friendly gatherings, a visit from a young writer or foreign student preparing a thesis on my work, everything exhausted me. Literary notoriety, too, was utterly devoid of interest. At the end of every sentence I uttered, or heard uttered by anyone else, between the lines of the page I was reading, inscribed as a sub-title on a cinema screen, or written on the walls or the ceiling, were the words: what's the good? Even sexual desire was weakened and corroded by the same thought: what's the good?

I told myself that I must go on living. And it was primarily as a sort of duty imposed on myself by myself that I went in for what are known as 'adventures'. The whole world seemed to me drab and muddy; I was incapable of fixing my mind on anything at all. People noticed, more than once, at social gatherings, that I wasn't there, that I was not listening to what was said to me. More than once they asked me definite questions to which I did not reply. I would ask for the same piece of information several times. Eating and drinking were the only things that had not lost their attraction, their flavour. And I was happy only when I was drunk. Unfortunately I had forgotten it all by next morning, I had no idea what this sort of happiness had consisted of. My body had become a burden too heavy to bear. I would open my eyes in the morning with a genuine pleasure in seeing the light of day; I would get up, and after a few minutes, weariness, like a leaden cloak, weighed me down. And behind it all, this thought: I am not living, life is passing by; and inside every fruit the inevitable kernel of anxiety, the idea of death. That has not disappeared, of course, one can't get rid of that so easily. It's as though in broad daylight I was seeing night: night mingled with day: 'the black sun of melancholy'.

And then, suddenly, came this joy about which I can only say that it is senseless. But it's got to be accepted as such; one must admit that happiness can only be senseless, and yet live it intensely. I must say that sometimes, during these last few years, a promise, a hint of happiness used to light up the bleak sky for me; I would meet it by saying to myself 'What's the good?' 'What does it mean?' or 'That won't prevent me from dying,' or 'There's no reason to be happy'; and the gleam of happiness faded out instantly and I was back in my greyness. The time, I seemed to understand that joy is a gift from heaven, it is like grace, inexplicable but evident and sure. It cannot be explained, there is no reason for it, and that must be its reason, and this absence of a reason may perhaps be the only valid, possible, true reason. This can be understood if I say to myself that all the reasons by which we explain anything at all are wrong reasons or untrue ones, since we know nothing and our intelligence is limited. I am thus reduced to admitting what has often been said before, that ignorance is the cause of our suffering, perhaps indeed the very substance of it.

Since we cannot be anything other than ignorant, there's only one solution: to ignore ignorance and act with confidence, as though we knew.

And in that lightheartedness that I felt yesterday the world appeared to me in a different light, a wholly new light. It was as if the trees and houses, people's faces, the water and the sky had all been cleansed, as if everything had become spotless, renewed and refreshed. But above all that sense of cleanness. And I felt that the world was becoming once again, had become, interesting, intensely interesting. What had I been doing all this while? Where had I been? Who had prevented me from looking and seeing? And indeed every particle of that world seemed to me full of the greatest interest. My own inner universe seemed fresh and virginal; I was renewed inwardly, my world was enfranchised or rejuvenated. When I change, I change the world. If only it would last! If only it would stay clean! If only this freshness could endure for ever, never be soiled again!

R.: poor dear little scrap of a thing, little scrap of a creature, burdened with anxiety, distress and love. I see her scurrying from one end of the flat to the other, like a squirrel, from one shelf of my bookcase to the other, tidying, classifying, looking for the object, the pencil or spectacles that I've just lost for the hundredth time in half an hour. The house is like a huge domain for her, who's so tiny, like an ant, meticulously busy, setting everything to rights. It's in my study that she feels most at ease, when she's sorting my letters and putting my manuscripts in order. There she feels happy. This is her domain, even more than the rest of the house. This is her universe, or rather the centre of her universe, the air she can breathe. I myself am her domain, I am as it were the place where she dwells. If I tell her to stop sorting my belongings or my papers, if she feels she's irritating me, she collapses. It's as though I were trying to drive her out of her own home. Indeed, this is where she's at home. I am her dwelling. Where else could she go and live? Her behaviour is surely genuine, authentic, since it's irrational. It is not logical, it's not conventional, it is profound, deep-rooted in a kind of universal, permanent truth. How can we alter anything? Can we shift the sun from its place, can we remove the sea or the earth from the universe? Can we do away with daylight, can we replace the four points of the compass by three? If I go away, if I withdraw myself, everything collapses. Poor loving creature who hates and yet adores me; I am her house, built by herself for herself.

To make her admit that every creature needs its independence, that as Rilke said the finest present one can give a loved one is freedom, is inconceivable to her; she does not understand the words independence, autonomy, something one's own that one needs to preserve. She feels no such need, she does not know the meaning of independence, since she belongs entirely to another and that other belongs to her. I feel a vital need for freedom; she cannot understand this, since for her freedom is something shared.

Jealousy is a fault, they say; don't be jealous, it's wrong to be jealous. But jealousy holds the world together. Human beings are jealous from the day they are born; cats are jealous, dogs are jealous, doves are jealous, and a tiger is as jealous as a tiger. Flowers are jealous, so are trees; God is jealous. One's jealous because one cannot live without love. She is jealous because there is one single being who can give her love, and from whom she can accept the love which she cannot help demanding from him. It's impossible to deprive her of love. It's impossible to prevent her from breathing, it's impossible not to love her, for not to love her would be to kill her. That's why I am obliged to love her. Of course one must be jealous, but not be possessed by jealousy. It's all a question of proportion.

But is it her fault if her heart is greater than herself? She feels more passion than she can contain. She is like a river that overflows because its bed is too narrow.

In short, H. said about his wife, she was quite right not to admit that I was right. If one starts understanding the other person, if one puts oneself in the other person's skin, one's done for, one is defeated. Each of us has his own reasons; if I take into consideration the other person's reasons, even in the slightest degree, I am caught up in the irreversible machinery of defeat. And defeat is what I mean, for it wasn't a question of discussing things and coming to an understanding, of weighing the pros and cons in friendly fashion, of trying to see as objectively as possible what could be done, whether some settlement could be made. There could be no settlement, no bargain; there was nothing to settle, this was a battle. She never disarmed, for to disarm would have been to succumb. One had to allow her to be in the right, unreservedly and on every plane. I thought I might have justifications and reasons; in her own eyes, she needed no sort of justification or reason, because she was reason incarnate. 'We are neither good nor bad' was for her an utterly untenable assertion. She believed in a rudimentary and absolute moral code. In good, which she always did, and in evil, which others were therefore bound to do. Basically, she was not completely taken in by it; but her belief in 'morality' was an important defensive weapon, since she assumed morality was on her side. Often she would weep to prove her case. She would weep, too, because she felt depressed, unhappy, hurt, she was moved by self-pity, which is quite legitimate since we live in a state of anxiety, since we need a great deal of love to enable us to go on living. S., more than anyone else, needed love. She was a living wound, from head to feet. I used to love her for that, and I shall love her again, I shall go back to her; if she needs love, one cannot not give it her. If I don't remember ever seeing her moved to pity by the sorrows, the anxieties, the needs of the other person, it's because these sorrows, these anxieties, these needs were due to his own fault and deserved only to be met with righteous indignation. As for her own faults, that's simple enough, they did not exist. (That's quite true; Hans had nothing to reproach her with.)

I had therefore no justification for the wrong I did her; or if she did allow me some semblance of an excuse, it was only to involve me more deeply in guilt; I was a victim, unfortunately, of my weakness, my lust, my vices. She probed no deeper into the causes determining human actions or states of mind, she made no further effort to elucidate moral notions, since her safeguard consisted precisely in not understanding. Society, as we know, defends itself with the rules of morality; this is also an individual's defensive weapon, a private shield.

But, Hans admits, how can you be understanding when you're on the defensive; your sole good, your hateful love is being torn from you, you're being flayed alive, stabbed to the heart and, at the same time, you are asked to understand the justifications of the person who is inflicting these mortal wounds on you. When I leave her I shall take away her skin, her life with me as well as my own. And both of us will be left incurable invalids.

We ought to have but one single thought, one aim: the other person's happiness; we ought all to fling ourselves at one another's feet.

We ought to consider ourselves and other people as we would a big fly battering itself against a window without knowing that one of the panes is open.

Oh yes, these are fine words!

We are comic. That's the way we should look at ourselves. Only humour, bland or black or cruel, only humour can give us back serenity.

I shall write no more dramas henceforward. I shall only write to amuse myself. I really ought not to write any more at all, but I have to make up plays and stories since I am a professional author, since that's my function. But really it's all worth very little. Literature is something derivative. What happened in the dream where I saw the wall? I did not climb over it nor pull it down, nor even try to pull it down, I walked round it; I keep on talking and talking and that absolves me from doing anything more. Literature brings me relief, it's an alibi, an excuse for not acting. I shan't write any more . . . except to construct objects, little make-believe worlds.

The bourgeois exploiter did not hate the proletarian whom he exploited. The Socialist states, so long as they are not weary or corrupt or decadent, hate their former exploiters, and the sons and grandsons of these former exploiters (everything seems to be turning into racism; in fact, the punishment of a single generation is not enough to satisfy the need for vengeance; the Bible tells us that the Hebrews, on their return from the Babylonian captivity, experienced a thirst for revenge and an understandable hatred for whatever was foreign, even the least bit foreign; thus not only were genuine foreigners impure but so was the Jew one of whose parents was foreign, and moreover in order not to be considered foreign the parents must not themselves have had a foreign parent; while the cattle and domestic animals belonging to the foreigner, and his servants, were also impure and had to be exterminated. His house, being impure, must be burnt down to the ground so that the stones might be purified.) But the totalitarian states hate and mistrust their own subjects, and those of them who refused to let themselves be exploited, that's to say alienated by renouncing their freedom, were sent off to be forcibly exploited in concentration camps, and sometimes indeed were forcibly alienated by extermination. Of course this process was not called exploitation of man by man, it was described as free enlistment or voluntary work undertaken out of zeal, whence the ironical expression 'voluntary forced labour'. It makes us laugh today, for the imposture is self-evident; but this was not the case even a short while ago, and if you told a progressive that all North Africans were not ready to die cheerfully for a freedom which they have not got and for which they no longer hope, now they have their independence, or that among the workers in Socialist Russia there was a single one who was not completely happy, the rich Parisian progressive would accuse you of being a reactionary, or in the pay of American capitalism, for this is the favourite indictment of advanced thinkers today, whose fathers, advanced intellectuals in their time, would have accused you of being in the pay of Moscow. But this is not exploitation; exploitation of man by man does not and cannot exist in Russia: the whole community is simply at the service of the state. And if you won't accept this, it means that we don't speak the same language. There is a bourgeois language (in which it is possible, after all, to disclose the exploitation of man by man) which corresponds to a bourgeois mentality; there is the new language which corresponds to the mentality and thought of the Revolution. Just you try to demystify that language! People will only shrug their shoulders. And it is this rudimentary insincerity that has given rise to what is known as the 'crisis of language', about which so many learned donkeys lecture us day and night. To revert to the exploiting bourgeois, he was not cruel, he was just indifferent. He did not hate the worker, he despised him, sometimes he felt sorry for him. And finally he himself developed a guilty conscience and abdicated, as the aristocracy had done previously. And today we see so many worthy people beating their breasts as they violently insult the bourgeoisie, that's to say themselves, whereas the bourgeoisie is no longer aggressive, has no longer the power to alienate, since the Trade Unions fortunately can defend themselves, while on the other side, as everyone knows, but as it must nevertheless be repeated, tyranny and exploitation are rife, although the press tries to hide it under propaganda's cartloads of bouquets. If the bourgeois had been lucid and far-sighted they could have said that the beginnings of industrial society required the sacrifice of the larger part of the population: the statement of this necessity would not have involved any trickery, nor any 'crisis of language'. I am not against the idea of Socialism, I am against what has been made of it: what the Russians have made of it; the failure of Socialism is entirely due to them. The task of achieving Socialism should never have been entrusted to a people with the hereditary taint of tyranny.

An incoherent dream, too disconnected, impossible to relate and moreover almost forgotten. I retain only these words: 'Here comes the sheriff,' spoken by a blonde woman; and I see the sheriff come in with his badge; the police, yet again. And I see a man with a black beard disappearing into the crowd.

People die of hunger. They die of thirst. They die of boredom. They die of laughing. They die of curiosity. They die of terror. They die in battle, of course. They die of sickness. They die of old age. They die every day.

Except for moments of ecstatic euphoria in adolescence, when I believed I was aware of absolute presentness, when I felt that everything was justified—more than that, redeemed—and except for the moments of fulfilment felt during my childhood at La Chapelle-Anthenaise, I have never experienced profound joy.

Of course my sadness that has no apparent reason, my despair, my distress were often covered over by moments of happiness (happiness is not joy) which to some extent filled that inner gulf: my engagement and marriage, fatherhood, professional satisfaction, that sort of notoriety which is partly pleasant and partly intolerable, all of this was important to me, and ensured transient forgetfulness without being able to solve anything at all, without being able to console me for the misfortune of feeling lost in a world that was doomed to death. I have never been able to master this overwhelming weariness, this vast psychological and physical weariness that I have borne on my back all my life long, and which has stopped me from ever rejoicing; I have felt ill at ease in life, all my life, not at home in it, surrounded by other people's misery as well as steeped in my own, and conscious that life is hellish, intolerable. People detest one another and so they can only find relief by killing one another, by rising up against each other, by telling lies and enduring suffering through other people in an effort to spare themselves suffering. Being neither a masochist nor a sadist nor a political fanatic, I believe I have always been lucid, with a simple and possibly inadequate sort of lucidity, but on the whole I have seen things straight. I understand why they fight, why they struggle, I understand why they refuse to understand, I am quite aware that the ideologies, philosophies and other reasons that they give themselves are only excuses and unconscious, or semi-conscious, justifications for their passions, for a secret despair . . . I know, and I also know that they will never admit it and will always refuse to demystify themselves, whereas there's so much talk today about demystification. A mind of superior lucidity would understand better not merely the reasons for unreason but, above all, the unreasonableness of reason. Such a mind would despise my limited, empirical sort of lucidity; I don't possess that superior lucidity which would give serenity. But it is surely better to be moderately lucid than to have no lucidity at all, than to be supremely duped, as are all those people who rush about talking and think they are thinking.

No, at no moment have I been able to feel at ease in this world of misfortune and death, for which I have felt powerless to do the slightest thing; all my actions turn out badly. The years have increased my depression, my weariness, my disgust and terror. So I have done my job, I said that there was nothing to say, I 'wrote', to use that painful term, I wrote with almost insurmountable distress, and the more amusing my writing appeared the more my unhappiness increased. I found it impossible to write comedies, or almost impossible; it was therefore in order to seek relief that I began writing gloomier dramas. I found a certain satisfaction in writing about misery and anguish; how can one talk of anything different when one is aware that one's going to die? Horror and rage at its mortality have made mankind what it is. Masochism, sadism, destruction and self-destruction, wars, revolts and revolutions, hatred of men for one another are provoked, consciously or not, only by the sense of our imminent end, and by the fear, transformed and transferred or not, of death. We do not feel well here, we do not feel at home. So long as our immortality is not guaranteed we shall remain unsatisfied and we shall go on hating one another in spite of all our need to love each other. Alas, how could such wretched creatures not fear everything from other wretched creatures? Each of us hates, in the other, his own mortality. Here's a saying: My children, mistrust one another.

And yet, and yet, there is the teaching of those admirable Hasidic rabbis who knew what love was, who knew how it could be attained, and from whom we could learn it again if we were not deaf and blind. The science of love. Neither to destroy one's enemies, for basically we have no enemies except by mistake, nor to run away from the earth, but to purify it, that's to say restore an awakened consciousness to men. To unite the relative to the absolute, to make our blindness put its trust in some wisdom. But blindness can never be anything else but blindness; the sadistic murderers accused these innocent preachers of love of killing Christian children to drink their blood; avaricious men, projecting their own shame on to these wise men, accused them of avarice, and Imperialists accused them of wanting to conquer the world.

Humanism, comfortable so-called humanism, the crude violence from which crude philosophies were made, the supposedly revolutionary aberrations, whose hatred is more consummate, more bitter, more cunningly fiendish, and being stealthy less easy to recognize than the stupidity of reactionary brutes, all this has been distilled, it permeates us, it exudes from us and returns to us, we build it up, we monumentalize it, and we call it 'culture'.

I have my own loathings, I am not immune from the epidemic, or rather the endemic, and in spite of it all, mingled with it all, a certain indifference which allows me to remain detached. For if I did not have this indifference, mingled with my anger, my anxiety, and thinning them down as water mixed with wine dilutes its strength, I could not even write this, I should tear up my sheet of paper, I'd smash everything. Dare I think that I don't hate for the sake of hating, that hatred is what I detest? But of course everybody detests hatred, and that's just why everybody has become so full of hate.

'Lie down on this couch, monsieur; that's right, just like that. Are you comfortable? Good. Breathe deeply. Breathe in, breathe out. Breathe naturally. Imagine that your arm has grown heavy, very heavy. Think: 'My right arm is very limp and heavy. My left arm is very limp and heavy. My arm is very heavy.' Imagine that your head is falling back a little. Keep your eyes tight shut. Imagine that your shoulders are light: 'My shoulders are so light.' Imagine that your right leg is heavy. Think: 'I am very relaxed and my leg is very heavy.' Both your legs are very heavy. Imagine that both your legs are very heavy. Think that you can feel your heart. Feel your heart beating. Think: 'My heart is beating slowly and regularly, my heart is beating gently and regularly.' Think that you can feel your stomach and your intestines. You can feel the blood circulating in your stomach. Say: 'I feel the blood circulating in my stomach and my intestines.' Imagine your pelvis is heavy, that it is pressed against the couch, that the couch is bearing its weight. Say: 'My pelvis is pressing into the couch.' Very good, now breathe naturally. Now breathe deeply, breathe in, breathe out. Open your eyes. Stretch yourself like a cat, pleasurably. You may yawn. Very good, monsieur, you've managed very well. Your pulse is far slower, it's beating normally. You'll have noticed, when I lifted your arm just now it dropped limply, it really had become heavy. There's something beautiful about a relaxed face and body. All the vital forces are there, at rest though not asleep. That's true relaxation. There's something very beautiful about a living body in a relaxed state.'

As he left the consulting-room they asked him: 'What's happened to you in the last half hour? You're smiling, you seem relaxed, you're quite changed, you seem so much younger.'

The monsters within him had rested, had relaxed, had yawned, and now they were ready to fly at other people with claws outstretched.

People don't change, their situations change. My circumstances can improve or grow worse but it's always myself in the midst of them, unchanged in my private essence. You can put a plant in the sun, and it'll grow; if you don't give it enough water, it fades; and yet, yellow or green, withered or blooming, it is always the same plant although its reactions to various conditions differ. The chameleon changes colour every time its self-protection requires it; does it therefore cease to be a chameleon? Does it become the surroundings that absorb it, does it become the leaf it imitates? It still remains the same chameleon. Thus, from the beginning, one is; one does not become; essence precedes existence; reactions differ, without altering that essence. History does not make us. Sometimes indeed we make it. Things do not make us, since we are already made. These things make us alternate between one state and another, but I recognize all of these states as being my own. I could not have been, I could never be, another person; whatever I may do, good or bad, I don't become that good thing, that evil thing, that truth or falsehood. It's not a question, then, of changing, but of recovering oneself: the unalterable element amid the temporary alterations of a self intermingled with the world. We tend to confuse changes of state and situation with some imaginary essential change. If I am in a state of irritation, of health or sickness, of well-being or discomfort, all that is really external to myself. If I were a labourer, a bourgeois, a workman, etc., I should be quite different from any other labourer, bourgeois, or workman, just as an actor remains the same through all his different roles. A cat does not become a cat, it is a cat from birth, it will behave like a cat and nothing can alter its cat's nature. It does not learn to be a cat, it knows how to be. I believe in the idea of a cat before the actual cat; I believe in the 'aprioric' cat. That is why, maybe illogically, I am inclined, in spite of everything, to believe that we are not debarred from immortality. This allows me to hope, too, that serenity and a sort of indifference will eventually prove stronger than my rage and despair. Eventually, human nature cannot be hateful. Its good or bad humour are temporary psychological changes, varying states which do not destroy it nor alter it essentially.

I believe I have been perfectly loyal to myself. I have not changed. Ever since I have known myself my feelings, my thoughts, my being have displayed an unvarying quality which events, life, have been unable to alter. I recognize myself in what I thought and was at seventeen. I never yielded to the lure of successive heresies and fanaticisms. Before discovering the answers, the reasons for my rejection of these, I resisted them stubbornly and spontaneously, without argument, without other reason than the mute and profound reason of my heart, leaving counter-arguments to be found later. I was what I was. I am what I have been. I learned to be alone very early, because I did not think what others thought. My deepest nature prevented me. But solitude is not isolation, it is not a barrier separating me from the world, it is a shield, a cuirass, which can defend my liberty, which allows me to keep a cool head in spite of the fiery furnace into which I am hurled by my rages, my repulsions, my terrors. I still communicate with others across the barrier, as far as is possible.

When I had told my mother that I was going to get married, she went to see my fiancée, and when the latter opened the door to her, my mother looked at her for a moment, although she had known her for quite a long time, as though she had an unfamiliar person in front of her; she looked at her with different eyes, as when one gazes at a landscape from a fresh angle which makes it seem like a strange landscape; a friend, the daughter of a friend, who was also a stranger, was becoming in some unexpected fashion her closest relative, as it were a daughter, as it were another myself, as it were another herself, someone she had been expecting from the beginning, whom she had foreknown, whom she did not recognize, and at the same time whom she seemed to have known since the beginning of time: the person appointed by fate, whom she was compelled to accept and yet had chosen. This was the princess, her heiress, soon to become queen in her stead. My future wife returned my mother's gaze; my mother had tears in her eyes but was restraining her emotion, and her quivering lips expressed a feeling beyond words. I don't know how far the two women were aware of what they were speechlessly saying to each other. It was a silent communication, a sort of brief ritual which they were spontaneously rediscovering and which must have been handed down to them through the centuries; it was a sort of handing over of powers. At that moment my mother gave up her place, and gave me up, too, to my wife. This was what my mother's expression said: he is no longer mine, he is yours. What silent injunctions, what sadness and what happiness, what fear and hope, what renunciation there was in this expression! It was a dialogue without words, in which I had no part, a dialogue between one woman and another.

This ceremonial lasted only a few instants, but it must have taken place according to rule, according to a very ancient law; and since it was a mystery, my wife acquiesced, joined in the sacred game and, obeying a will, a power that transcended them both, bound me to herself, bound herself to me for eternity. She has never tried to break away. She has never known any other man. I have sometimes sought to break away for a moment or more, but my escape seemed like sacrilege. My mother entrusted me to my wife, who assumed responsibility for me and who subsequently became my sole relative, more mother than my own mother, my sister, my perpetual betrothed, my child and my comrade-in-arms. I am sure this was how it happened, I am convinced that my wife, who took over responsibility for me, could never or would never have tried to relinquish it, and that this bond could never be broken because the sacred promise had been made.

My mother died three months after my marriage. I had an enormous love for her. I did not suffer at her death because I had a new family, my wife's mother, my wife; I was welcomed, sheltered, established, re-integrated. If I should seek to shatter this unity I could never make more than a few breaches, a few wounds; that I should foster other longings, that I should wish for another spring, another sun, dream of beginning life again, is impossible, is inconceivable, for the power of the mystery that has been accomplished is too great.

A cosmos has developed from this seed, has formed itself and I am the principal figure, the centre of this cosmos; there is no other world than this, it is a permanent datum; if I should no longer be there, at any rate mentally, it would mean a gaping hole, a chasm that would stretch to the edge of the world, engulfing everything. I don't believe my physical death, though it would surely work havoc, would destroy that world, but my spiritual absence would certainly put an end to it.

An Old Dream

A few years ago I was spending a holiday in England with my wife and daughter. We stayed for about a month with a friend, an Englishwoman. She had a very pretty house dating from the seventeenth century, with a wonderful garden. A more modern wing had been set aside for her guests; she lived at the opposite end, with her children. Next to the double room where we slept was a single room for my daughter. A few days after our arrival I had a strange and rather terrifying dream: I was surrounded by a whole ring of doctors in white coats. One of them told me: 'Monsieur, we shall have to operate on your brain.' 'That won't be pleasant, but if it's got to be done, go ahead.' Suddenly the doctors disappeared. One of them came back to tell me they had all made a mistake, that there was nothing the matter with me and I could go home. I found this suspicious and I begged the doctor to tell me the truth: 'I've a malign tumour on the brain that can't be operated on, that's why you want to send me home; tell me the truth, I implore you.' 'Well then,' the doctor said, 'if you really want to know the truth, that is the case, you have an incurable cancer on the brain.'

At this point I woke up in acute distress. It was dawn. I remembered a friend who had died long ago of a brain cancer; one of the symptoms of his illness was the loss of his sense of direction. If he wanted to go to the right, he found himself going left. When he tried to reach the door he would find himself by the window. I got up then, bathed in sweat, and to reassure myself, I tried to see whether I still had a sense of direction. I decided to go to the window; I reached it. I said to myself: 'Now let's go to the door'; I walked straight there without difficulty. This was a great relief. However, still under the influence of my fear, I went on walking about the room, making for various goals which I allotted myself one after the other. The bedside table, the other window, the wardrobe, the other wall, then the first wall again, and so on. My wife, whom all this to-do had woken up, opened one eye and in great surprise asked me if I had gone mad. I replied that I thought not, and explained why I was thus roaming round the bedroom. She told me it was crazy to take a nightmare so seriously. I went back to bed, but could not sleep. About nine o'clock, we went down for breakfast in the dining-room at the other end of the house. Our hostess and my daughter were down already. The latter challenged me: 'I heard you snoring through the wall, you snored very loud.' 'I couldn't have been snoring, for one thing I don't snore, for another I was not asleep.' 'Yes, you were snoring, and very loud too, a queer sort of snore.' I was about to protest when Mrs D. said to my daughter: 'Yes, dear, it was probably your father snoring.' I said nothing, but felt somewhat surprised. As soon as my daughter had left the room Mrs D. said to me: 'Forgive me, it wasn't you snoring, it was my grandfather. It was not a snore but a death-rattle. Every year, at the exact moment when he died, that death-rattle is heard. Don't worry, nothing else happens.' 'I know how and why your grandfather died,' I said. 'He died of a brain cancer, he'd been taken to hospital, they had wanted to operate and then decided not to, for as one of the doctors told him at his own request, the tumour was inoperable. That was why he died at home.' 'How do you know this?' asked Mrs D. 'It's quite true.' 'Because I dreamed it all last night,' I said.

Since this event, the death-rattle has never been heard again. It was as if I had taken it upon myself. The dead man gave no sign on August 8th either the next year or the year after. And Mrs D.'s parents, the daughter and son-in-law of the dead man, came back to live in that wing of the house, which they had left to build themselves another house some hundred and fifty yards away.

Last Night's Dream

A few scraps of images still linger in my mind. Gloomy colours, black and dark grey. I think I was in some old village, or some shabby dilapidated district on the outskirts of a town, with my maternal grandparents; it was a strange place, unfamiliar to me and, so it seemed, it was the place my grandparents had come from. I don't know how I had come there, certain things had happened and there had been discussions of which I retain only the vaguest memory. There were two of my uncles (one bearded) who are still living, and who are very old. I still have a picture of a low room on the ground floor with a wretched bed or two. Does someone tell me that my grandfather has died, or that he's dying, or that he's going to die? Am I told, or do I tell myself the same thing about my grandmother? I can see her as she was in her lifetime, dark, without a single white hair in spite of her great age. I find myself at the town hall of this village or suburb, at the Registry Office; several clerks are there, I speak to one of them, a youngish fellow. I am glad to be there, this is perhaps why I have come, to find out the real name of my grandmother's mother, her maiden name which none of us knew, perhaps because she kept it a secret: something compromising about my great-grandmother's social origin? Did she belong to some persecuted or ostracized ethnic category? But I am bent on finding out my origin. The clerk tells me that I can only learn my great-grandmother's name at the Town Hall of the tiny village where we now are, for it is the only village in the world that still possesses all the archives relating to everybody, whether or not they originally came from the place.

As I saw her in my dream, in the old low house, my grandmother's appearance was deplorable: very badly dressed, almost like a female tramp, filthy and ragged. Suddenly I see her outside in a little yard surrounded by a low stone wall. The ground is hardened mud, the sky still dark, the houses all around low and grimy. But there's my grandmother, grown young again, wearing a lovely light dress, beautiful, quite changed, surrounded by a crowd of children, her children; actually she had had twelve. She has grown young again because she has changed her name which kept her apart from the world and forced old age upon her. By changing her name she inevitably recovered her youth. I look at her and I am seized with an indefinable feeling of anxiety, this ought not to be or cannot be, or perhaps a sense that it was not quite proper. To my right, on the right side of the yard, a little tumbledown one-storey house, which might have been the same house seen from outside, and into which one of my two old uncles goes; he is very ill. The minute he goes into the house, fire breaks out. The house is ablaze, flames soar up; the firemen in their red uniforms appear, driving a red engine.

I never saw the end of the fire, nor the new house that replaced the old one which was burnt down. I never managed to find out the name of my grandmother's mother, the name I was searching for. I am still searching for that name. . . .

Our friend Sorana Gurian died some years ago after a serious illness. Day after day, for months, for a whole year or two, injections kept her alive, granted her a reprieve from one day to the next.

Michel M., the psychotherapist, thought that the anguish in which Sorana lived was cruel and intolerable. He decided to do something for her, to help her as best he could. He went to the nursing home one day, then the following day, then every day for two or three months. He had resolved to teach Sorana how to die, to teach her death. He succeeded in this difficult undertaking. One morning, Sorana calmly told the doctor who came to give her the daily injection that she did not want it, that she did not want to be put to sleep, so that she might keep her consciousness intact until the last moment. A week later she died, with dignity, as she had wished to.

Z. tells me: psychologists have always been familiar with premonitory and clairvoyant dreams. We cannot believe in them, in the West, because for us events take place in time. Our thought is causal: there is a before and an after, the latter resulting from the former. Before, after: causality, time. Eastern thought, which we reject, is not understood in the West, for Eastern thinkers see things in a complex of correlations and meanings. It is clearly a different way of interpreting the world, any truth being merely the interpretation we may give of a thing, of things. To admit these phenomena which seem to us strange or absurd, we should simply have to substitute for our historic, causal way of thought a spatial way of thought. We should imagine things spatially, not temporally. If we could abandon our historical point of view without assuming a spatial one, we should be even freer, we should have a different figuration of the world or rather, since any figure is in space, a non-figurative interpretation of the world.

Once again, do I really want salvation?—I was going to say: do I really want to be saved? but that suggests 'seeking safety', 'running away'. Do I really want to fulfil myself, to know myself really? To be truly master of my life and of my death, or else do I simply want to produce, to go on producing, literature?

Then the season was autumn. Time abolished duration, implausible as that may seem. My pockets were full of my happiest days. A highly inconvenient situation, from which I might hope to reap benefits; I was a walking money-box. I might prove insolvent, but I could afford that. 'What's the good of it' is turning nasty, I said to myself. Other thoughts crossed my mind: 'The grave's a nasty place.' 'Periodicity is temporary, time gets its sap from space.' 'Space is not an empty word, for emptiness is not space.' 'One can't say of a thing that it is, for that thing is what it is, as everyone knows: but one can and must assert that it is not.' 'No hair-set is erudite.' Careless as a bird over the bare fields or a cock on the crest of the waves, I hummed songs that were perfectly senseless, such as this one:

Nicotine wastes time, nicotine gnaws bread.

(This is untrue, I know, like almost everything that is devoid of meaning, for we are well aware that on the contrary bread gnaws nicotine and thyme wastes it.)

But now, in wet weather, the mist breaks up. A sudden lightning flash streaks the horizon; I hurried to my dentist's.

Other thoughts crossed my mind. The rain was pouring down. Where were the parishioners sleeping? Where was the Mayor buried? What did the Supervisor advise?

The duck came up, like a rose tree in plume. I watched her come, goggle-eyed, ringing bells on her toes and buttercups on her backside. 'Why?' she quickly asked me. 'Broad as you are, what are your salamanders?'

'Roast or raw?' I replied. 'Roast or raw, why don't you answer? Why do you wear curlers in your hair?' 'To make it curl.' The illogicality of her reply would have made me laugh, but for that ever-accelerated wailing.

'Around and around,' I cried, 'around you, around us, around our children!'

Vexed, she retorted: 'It's not the end of the week.'

'Hallelujah here, panorama there, my dear!'

'You're grieving, my love!'

'Yes, I'm grieving, maybe,' I said to her, 'but do the echoes grieve?'
She stood speechless. Where had she bought that fur coat?

'You see, my dear, these lilies are lilac. Don't let's stop there. Your
neck, if you don't mind.'

We tucked up our arms and decamped. Moved away. The plushy
lawns were stuffed with creepers. The eagles went to sleep, but the
sentry was watching: how nice we were!

Galloping over the drawbridge. Horseflesh-eaters skedaddled.
Dandelions first, free of coverlets or controversy. They took off. My
jaw itched. Our jaws itched. An invasion of hippopotami or calves.

To the sound of bells, to the rolling of thunder, topsy-turvy, all
the winds of the air, at top speed, tall candles—blue, red, green, black,
brown, white, blue, green, black, brown, red, blue, orange, black,
orange, yellow, green, red, blue, multi-sonorous, O those tall unending
candles, o dear, o dear, o dear, the clytemnestras were converted! O dear
o dear o dear, you needn't go on saying it. Everybody has gone away.

Other thoughts crossed my mind.

It's almost a year since I practically broke off this journal and this quest, this exploration in the tangled impenetrable forest in search of myself. For the time being I don't feel I have made any progress, done anything constructive, made any decision. I feel that I have only succeeded in discovering what I already knew. Moreover, it's an open question whether there is anything to discover, or anyone, whether there is a hidden soul that might reveal itself. Perhaps there is nothing else but these tangled thickets, these thorns, this dry rock. Perhaps that's what the soul is: a place where all sorts of things, all sorts of forces simply take up the ground. Perhaps there are nothing but happenings, conflicting events, shadows. No psyche, just a psychic life like a field for intersecting forces. Nobody. The self, then, would be nothing but a knot of conflicting principles in dynamic equilibrium. I untie this knot, the forces are dissipated, there is nothing left. Perhaps nothing but movements.

But there is this anxiety. That may be a sign that there is a being, and that this being reacts.

What is there to discover, what is there to know? Is there any advantage in knowing anything? Perhaps, after all, I have reclaimed a few square yards of virgin forest. If I had reclaimed a little more I should only have pushed back the boundaries of the unknown, that unknown that recedes as I draw nearer to it.

To integrate the shadows; to elucidate. What a painful task! I wonder if it is in my power, this task that demands a constant effort to attain what? The black, dense mass, the wall will always be there behind every wall we throw down. If only someone would push me, send me rolling down into the abyss. Being trustful means letting oneself go. I am mistrustful. The current bears me away nevertheless, in spite of my protests, although I try to cling to the banks. I am carried away willy-nilly and as I don't want to let myself go it hurts me when it happens.

I dream that I am walking alongside the wall of a barracks. I pass in front of the barracks door. Through it I catch sight of the main buildings, which are a gloomy dark grey, almost as gloomy as the colour of the sky. A soldier is coming out, or has already come out of the barracks yard. I am walking behind him. I accidentally knock up against him. He turns round. I apologize. He is very dark-skinned, a mulatto or a Hindu perhaps. On his left cheek there's a scar. It must be Schäffer again. He does not accept my apologies. He's stubborn. My words do not reach him. Meanwhile I walk past him. He's behind me, he gives me a great blow in the back of the neck to punish me, to revenge himself, for he thinks I knocked up against him on purpose to show my contempt for him. And even if I did not do it on purpose it was none the less a sign of contempt.

This soldier is as impenetrable, as pitiless as a wall, as the barracks wall that stretches out endlessly. The same blind force or law, the same incomprehensible fate; that absolute, closed, limited order with which I cannot communicate. Who is this figure? I don't know if it is my other self, or simply other people. In any case this is surely the obstacle which I invariably knock up against: a dangerous, possibly stupid stranger to whose law I am subject. He is himself the embodiment of some law. A military policeman; a soldier rather than a policeman, for he does not represent conscience or morality, he is deaf and blind like the wall.

I recognize this house. I had not come here for a long time. But I have been here many times in my dreams. On the slope, almost at the foot of the hill, at the crossing where the muddy lanes meet, it's the house where I lived with my mother. The atmosphere is gloomy. It's a small white house, with one room, mine, looking on to the hillside, its window almost at ground level; a passage separates my room from the kitchen, which is always rather dirty, full of grimy pots and pans. On the other side of the passage there's my mother's room and possibly a third.

I always feel uneasy when this house appears in my dreams. Some time ago it was sunk still deeper into the ground, like a basement with damp walls and slits for windows. This house is always on the point of sinking in, of being flooded, of falling to pieces. It is threatened on all sides.

Had I come to visit my mother? My wife is with me as I stand in front of this house. She is sometimes herself, sometimes my mother, sometimes herself and my mother both at once. My daughter is with us too, and she is alternately, or at the same time, as big as she is today and as small as in the days when we must have lived in this dream house, six years old. Towards the end of the dream she becomes definitely small again and my wife ceases to be my mother. I say: 'Why, yes' (trying to combat a certain pessimism, my own as much as theirs) 'we were very happy when we lived in this house. Very happy. The house was clean, we kept it warm with stoves that defied the damp. Even though there was still some dampness in the clay walls it was a warm, comfortable dampness. We had friends.' We had wanted to revisit the house, and after going through the inside we come out again. The earth is muddy in the lanes, a dark brown colour. On either side there are grassy meadows and trees, but the sky is overcast and the leafy trees and the grass are very dark. With my wife and my little girl, whom I am holding by the hand (is there someone else? I think so, yes, the vague slender silhouette of a man, a vague voice) we go up one of the lanes, the one that leads to the top of the hill. We find walking difficult because the earth clings to the soles of our shoes.

I knew where we would get to if we went on walking. I remember, in my dream, the town I have seen in several other dreams, which stands at the top of the hill: a little town, with low houses amid gardens, decent but humble little houses. Beyond it I know, too, that there's a train running from the top of the hill to the other hill, with the rails suspended over the void, without sleepers, for part of the way. But this aerial journey belongs to another dream. My daughter tells me that she knows the way very well. That's the way we often used to go, she tells me, to get to Fabrègue (was that the name?). Then I remember it too. After that the lane gets very narrow, the hedges lining it grow tall, the earth is damp and the sky still very dark.

We go back to our old house to have a last look at it before leaving. Something has changed. It is still our house, and yet it's no longer standing by itself, another house on the hillside is built close against it. We go further down the lane to look at the front of our house: it's the same and yet not the same; does it have an extra floor? The windows of the upper storey are a more graceful shape, the house has become quite white, the windows are all lit up, the lights are on inside the house and yet there is no one there. I discover that the light comes from a fire, the flames are ravaging the inside of the house. The house is all white, the windows are flame-coloured against the dark, gloomy landscape and the sky is almost black.

What a flood of images, words, characters, symbolic figures, signs, all at the same time and meaning more or less the same thing, though never exactly the same, a chaotic jumble of messages that I may perhaps end by understanding but which tells me no more about the fundamental problem: what is this world? What is it that's all around me? Who am I? Is there an 'I' and if there is an 'I' where am I going? What am I doing, what am I doing here, what am I to do? I have been asking myself these questions from the beginning, I have always been at the foot of the wall, I have always been in front of a locked door. There is no key. I am waiting for the answer whereas I ought to provide it myself, to invent it. I keep waiting for a miracle which does not come. Presumably there is nothing to understand. But one's got to have a reason, to find a reason. Or else to lose one's reason.

She flings open my bedroom door, in this place where I have come to be cured. She opens it wide, and I am scarcely surprised to see her. She looks very well and very young. 'Don't tell anybody I'm here, not even the nurse.' She comes into my room because it is her own room and because I am her home, her room.

I will open the door of my heart to her, even wider. She must come in, I must let her come in. She can't have the door of her home shut against her.

A very short dream. A coloured picture. In a vast field, I am standing in an open waggon gliding gently along railway lines; above, the vault of heaven, very pure and blue, and to left and right of me green grass. Far ahead of me, a yellow field of corn blending into the sunlight. A narrow, bare path streaking across the landscape.

I am the accused and at the same time the prosecutor. Standing in the dock, I am speaking in my own defence. Am I also speaking for the prosecution? No, that's somebody else. The accused-prosecutor is a short, squat man with a red face, vociferating in front of the prisoners in the dock—an array of dark-coloured vegetables; sweet potatoes, beetroot, lettuce, like a market stall, with the colours of the earth.

The accused-prosecutor attacks one woman because she had borne false witness against the society of her country in certain political trials, saying that everything was going well there and that the accused had been slandering her country. This was why he was being tried. But the accused defends himself vehemently. The woman with whom he is arguing has black hair, she is thin and wears a black shawl over her head.

I remember another dream in which I was quarrelling with a woman from whom I wanted to buy vegetables which she refused to sell me. The same thin woman with black hair. Obviously the accused-prosecutor is myself, but who is the woman, and what are those vegetables doing here?

I am a murderer, I have killed children. I am not the only person accused; Beckett, too, is accused, as well as a third dramatist, Pinter maybe or Genêt, whom I see melting away and vanishing into a grey cloudless sky. Beckett acknowledges his crimes, he is unrepentant, hard-faced, he will kill more children if no one stops him. But I am seized with remorse, ravaged by an overwhelming sense of guilt. And yet I have killed no children. Or else I have killed them unintentionally. Or else I may have wanted to kill them, for who does not sometimes want to kill children? But I never carried out my intentions. The proof is that each time I felt tempted to kill children, or killed any by mistake, I sent for the police myself. And precisely, here comes the Black Maria, the police car, in answer to my summons. Here it is in front of me, and on my right a plot of newly-sown soil on the bank of the Seine. From the earth shoots are emerging, and even tiny white flowers with a green leaf, lilies of the valley.

He had clumsy shoes, poor fellow. He had so often been jeered at on account of those shoes, poor dad. He didn't like his shoes, so here we were behind the post office, the main post office, both of us, a crowd of us. His second wife, his daughter-in-law, his brother-in-law Michou and Tanase are all dead. I'm very sorry for my father, he is alive although he died nineteen years ago. What has happened to that pack of cards? He's as dead as they are, he died with them, and yet here he is alive, alone, alone and sad, he didn't belong to their world. There's a crowd between the post office and the junk shops, close to the Dambovitza, the Dambovitza or the Seine. Which is it, the Seine or the Dambovitza? It's the main post office, you poor old idiot. Well, now, we need a car, a taxi to get to the restaurant. I go along that narrow passage where I know there is a taxi rank, it's the corridor in a hospital, on my left is the Seine, I have to step over the old hospital patients, and at the end of the passage there's a cul-de-sac; you can't go any further; so I go back to my father amongst the crowd between the main post office and the junk shops, close to the Dambovitza or the Seine.

They're dead, I tell you, and so's my mother, and your mistress, and that ass of a captain, that fool of a Buruiana, oh Dad, you poor old idiot!

In my dreams there is, there is, there is a crowd close to the river, there is a painter on the bank of the Seine. He tells me: this is the year 1938, can you imagine 1938, it's still a revolutionary time. The spirit of 1789 is still alive in these people. . . . France still exists, these good folk believe in it, the painter said. This is 1938, how lively and intelligent the French are, fortunately this is 1938 and we haven't yet reached 1945. Look at the French in 1945, how stupid they are, how defeated! Aren't their intellectuals a set of despicable idiots, in 1945? I'm standing beside the Seine, with my luggage, waiting for a train or a metro to get to my hotel, in 1938, when Paris was alive, or in 1945 or 1950, by which time Paris was dead. The swan song . . . the song of a swan on the dirty

Seine, not knowing whether it is 1938 or 1950. I put down my luggage on the river bank and I wait, I wait. . . . Someone will have to come and take it all away.

It's a bewildering situation. There are several members of my family there, huddled close together. I am with my wife, my six-year-old daughter, my mother, my father, my aunt, a grandmother? I discover that my mother, who's talking to me, is not my mother but my wife, who tells me that since my mother is dead, my daughter is an orphan; we are clustering together on the platform of a moving vehicle. My daughter is six years old in this vision but she is quite unlike my real daughter, she has a white face and a great black Oriental eye, like an Egyptian figure. On hearing of the death of my mother, who is now replaced by my wife, I experience a great grief; making a great effort I remember that she died nearly thirty years ago, nearly thirty years ago. I see a great hole, and I feel dizzy, and my grief is ten times greater; alone, all that time, alone without my darling mother; then another lady is telling me about my mother's death, about my father's; my father? he is dead, but I'd seen him the day before (he died eighteen years ago in fact); I feel terribly unhappy, and besides if, as my wife, or this lady, keep telling me, my daughter is an orphan, does it mean that my wife is dead too? I don't feel very sure and I wonder if it's my father who is dead or myself. We go on travelling. A few heads fall off, like grapes from a cluster. In a few moments of dreaming I discover that I have lost all the members of my family, one after the other. How could I not have known it, or how could I have understood it so inadequately, without suffering that aching emptiness of which I now become so powerfully, so clearly conscious? Life cannot go on as it did before. This is all happening out of doors, in a dark landscape, with a forest. The platform of the funicular on which we are all travelling, both the living and the dead, shakes as it descends. On the right there's a low house, the colour of clay. Is that the cavern that's going to engulf us all?

I shall certainly never come back to this nursing-home. The cult of vegetarianism: a sort of second-rate religion, a bogus

asceticism, a mean and meanly hypocritical moral code. 'Naturism.'
I have been here two weeks and my behaviour surprises them all.
Not to be like everyone else, to be a sick man, to be feeling ill, is
considered shocking. This is a nursing-home for healthy people,
or for those with sensible illnesses. I'm having a fit of depression,
a nervous reaction. I have to leave, all the same. They would have
kept me if I had had an ordinary illness, a healthy illness, for of
course not being mediocre is a crime, it is *the* crime. And yet
Dr L., the carrot fairy, is not a bad doctor. 'There's not much the
matter with you,' she tells me, 'your body is reacting favourably'
(in spite of the nervous depression!) 'it's your psychology that's all
wrong.' She says this in a tone that makes me realize that it is
unforgivable for one's psychology to be all wrong. You've got to
live according to Nature. What do they mean by Nature?
For Dr L., Nature really means mediocrity and nothing more,
which implies stupidity, blindness and hypocrisy. This Boy Scout
morality is surely not Nature, but a defence-mechanism against
Nature: Nature is danger, it is volcanoes in eruption, storms,
cyclones, abysses, danger, death, the impossible state of our existence, almost hell, at any rate not heaven. One can't stop here
too long, in any case, they can't keep you too long, for the first
few days are the most profitable for the nursing-home, it's during
the first week that you have the most expensive analyses. You can
see the old fox's photo on the little brochures that are handed out
to the guests in this lousy hotel. A prophet of stupidity, of
pseudo-moral moralizing that conceals a more basic immorality.
Dr L. despises everything that is not mediocre. But medicine it-
itself, and psychotherapy, were more or less invented by people
who were not mediocre; they are constantly being improved by
people whose inner anxiety impels them to action. I ask Dr L.:
'What do you do if someone who's in this nursing-home for a
fortnight has a collapse on the thirteenth day?' She replies: 'We
manage, we send them to a nursing-home.' So this is not a nursing-
home, it's a hotel which is very expensive and where they practise
a dubious, out-of-date therapy, based on a stupid sort of wisdom,
a bogus wisdom that claims to cure everything, a bogus asceticism
and a dietetic theory. The cure-all food is a dish consisting mainly
of apples. All this raw stuff is bad for the stomach and guts;

and diabetics are forbidden to touch apples; so Dr L. has written a whole book to explain that all kinds of fruit are good, even and particularly for diabetics. I find it hard to believe in the scientific objectivity of this apple-woman. They sell a lot of apples in this house, which battens on the credulity of the worthy folk who put their trust in health through mediocrity. The buildings go up, the kitchen-gardens flourish, trade is good, the house prospers, but the charwomen get starvation wages and the diet is profitable, since food costs nothing! The house is run by the old fox's daughter, an ugly little woman as lean as a rake who, so they tell me, is an excellent and ruthless administrator. Ruthless: if anyone needs to stay two days longer, there's nothing to be done about it, other clients are coming to pay high fees and contribute to the boundless enrichment of the undertaking. May I add that professional secrecy is not always observed? Is it indispensable for doctors and nurses to tell each other everything about the sick people who come to be cured? I speak to Dr Z. about the futility of my staying here, for I could quite well have massage at home or elsewhere, get analyses done in any laboratory and prepare my carrots myself. Z. is a psychologist, and I thought he would have understood. I tell him all I think about the cupidity of those who run the place. I tell him the myth needs debunking. I tell him it wouldn't be quite so serious if there weren't such immorality behind this humbug, if there weren't such contempt for all that is not contemptible, if there were anything other than an excessive respect for that which deserves no respect: conformity, an anti-spiritual attitude, a failure to understand human nature, in other words all the defects that doctors ought not to have.

Z. asks me whether I intend to publish the criticisms I have confided to him. I tell him, yes. He replies that I must take care, be prudent, it might be awkward for me. They would not hesitate to go to law, he says. So he's threatening me. It's all right to criticize God, but the despicable, greedy petty bourgeoisie and its far-from-disinterested healers must not be criticized.

I suddenly get a glimpse into Z.'s soul. Is this mind-healer blackmailing me? How can I have wasted so much time here! If at least my experience could serve as a warning to those who might be tempted to try mediocrity as a cure! I myself feel increasingly ill at ease here. Only my anxiety is growing and flourishing. Banality is not a good shield, you can't hide your eyes behind it. The bogus austerity and asceticism, the Boy Scout moral code, to which are added the wealthy administration's insatiable greed for gain, only intensify my distress; they only intensify all my ills. Everything rises to the surface again. All my problems revive. All my ghosts revisit me, father, mother, all the rest. And the basic anxiety. These problems are personified; that does not mean they are soluble. The more living they are, the less they can be solved. And yet I shall go on trying, I mustn't give up. It might become interesting, I might see light tonight. To succeed in knowing oneself, however little, in knowing which way to go oneself, means beginning to know the world and which way the world is going. But all this is nothing but words as yet, no, not entirely since there is still that literally unbearable anxiety. And it's beginning all over again. Getting drunk doesn't help, nor does the Swiss psychologist. Not strong enough.

At the end of the dream about my father, when I saw that he was wearing black boots like mine or rather that mine were like his, I laughed and we both laughed. I had made a concession to him. This was a dream of reconciliation. I felt that he was alone, living among all these dead, at a loss, bewildered, out of the world. A whole world, all those who surrounded him, in the abyss.

What was the point of all the vegetables, and dark fruits, and seeds, and the soil? Shoots. It seems as if there were two levels of censorship: one in our waking life which represses symbols, and one actually within our dreams which makes those dreams only disclose part of what they could and would like to disclose. A dream-censor. There is an unconscious within the unconscious: there is something in dreams that seems to be thrusting through, like those seeds, secretly, barely perceptibly, as though dreams stressed what was least important in order to take one in, to hide what is essential, and the essential only appears in a corner of the background, in spite of the dream-censor, against his censorship. That's what I should like to understand, the meaning of those tiny things, those elements, those seeds which are barely sprouting.

To know what there is beneath it all. That's the most important thing.

These walls that rise up, these impenetrable walls which I so doggedly seek to bring down or to break through may perhaps represent reason. Reason raised these walls to preserve us from chaos. For behind these walls there is chaos, there is nothingness. There is nothing behind these walls. They are the frontier between what we have managed to make of the world, and the void. On the other side there's death. Keep this side of those walls.

Within me, there's hell. I know what hell is now.

A boundless night. A sort of nebula, a sort of round, dimly glowing light, a glow that gives no light, a globe about to break up: or a birth. Is this a sign that nothingness is about to resume possession, or is it a germ, a birth? The end is like the beginning.

I am divided between love of myself and love of the other. That's my drama, that's my hell. Incapable of giving myself up for the sake of others, incapable of giving up others for my own sake. I ought to tell myself, I ought to be convinced that neither others nor myself are of much importance. Of any importance at all. In vain I tell myself this, I cannot bear to deprive others of the love I owe them. I cannot deprive myself. Well, it can't go on for very much longer.

There is a sort of asceticism here, all the same, Dr Z. told me. There are just a few restrictions, easily tolerable, not actually fasting but just a lighter diet. 'It seems to you like a barracks,' he went on. 'It's a pampered sort of barracks,' I answered, 'a barracks for the rich: ugly but comfortable.' And expensive. To be poor in Switzerland, so they tell me, and I can see it's true, is a sin, it's immoral. Wealthy people are entitled to privileged treatment, to honour and reward them for being rich. On the other hand the poor are punished. They ought to be, and they are; there's another sanatorium for poor people a little farther off in the forest, run by the same family. There they are strictly disciplined; they sleep in

communal dormitories; they have to take their exercise all together, march in close ranks, sing while they march, often barefoot in the grass, they take their sauna baths in common whereas
in the rich people's nursing-home baths and massage are taken in
discreet privacy. In a word, it's a punitive system, a barracks, it's
collectivism. The poor don't deserve any consideration. This, and
not any sort of asceticism, is what makes it a barracks. As under a
totalitarian régime, there are privileged individuals and there is
the mass, who aren't treated so nicely, who are subjected to a
hygienic and moral discipline which is not quite that of a concentration camp but is essentially akin to that.

I find myself in a place that is hard to describe. There are two or
three dark rooms. It's impossible to make out the shapes of the
furniture in the gloom. A few outlines, shadows, confused voices,
people speaking to you whom you cannot see clearly. The rooms
open out on to a road where the earth is baked hard. I lead a
dark, elderly woman—perhaps my mother, although she doesn't
look very like her—into the biggest room in the house. I make
her sit down in an armchair with a black back. She seems cheerful
enough, treats me affectionately. I go a few steps towards the
door, and turn my head before I reach it. The expression on her
face has suddenly altered. She looks tense with anxiety and at the
same time angry with me. Her eyes have grown fierce, under her
black hair. Her dress is black too. She has a black bag that bursts
open and lets fall quantities of tiny white pills. They are poison-
ous pills. I hold her bag upside down and empty it. Dozens,
hundreds of white pills roll out on to the dark floor and even on
to the road in front of the house. I pick them up, I prevent her from
picking them up, I've got to pick them all up, one after the other,
there mustn't be one left. On hands and knees I search all over the
floor, under the table, in every corner, out on the road. She
mustn't have a single one back, for each of these minute pills is
dangerously powerful. The woman glares fiercely at me and
abuses me.

A few scraps of images. I am looking at a thin woman wearing
a hat, carrying a handbag. She is dressed in black; she may have a

necklace. This woman has grown feeble-minded with age, for at one point some relative of hers tells me 'we all *tip over*, in our family'. This woman used to have excellent manners. She is thirty-five or maybe forty years old. I myself think she still has pretty good manners. She is the producer of one of my plays, the production of which I have just been watching, for this seems to be taking place in a theatre. M. is playing the principal part, which he hasn't had time to learn. I try to understand what he is saying, but he only pretends to speak, he utters meaningless or pointless words. I get annoyed, and go away. People come up to me. M. apologizes and explains that there wasn't time, that they had to put the play on in a great hurry to take advantage of the lady's money, which she might have taken back.

M. and somebody else confirm the fact that all members of this woman's family go crazy ('tip over') at a certain point. The whole family are very wealthy, they own a whole district of the town. When one member of the family goes crazy, tips over, he loses his share, his property goes to rack and ruin, the houses become dilapidated and threaten to collapse. Then the other members of the family (particularly a certain uncle), who haven't tipped over yet, buy back the share that was being ruined, and rebuild it so that the wealth may stay in the family. Apparently this uncle is the only one who has not tipped over.

I am shown on a map of the town the whole vast district that belongs to them, with black marks, crosses, on the portions that were in danger of ruin. Black lines across the map strike out all those that have been redeemed, salvaged. I am also shown all that would be lost if the lady who is producing my play were to tip over completely. The uncle has surrounded the whole thing with a barbed wire fence which is shown on the map. How much longer is it going on? How much longer?

This lady used to be intelligent and polite. Now she is merely polite, she's no longer intelligent, she does silly things. Her good manners may still take one in. Then, suddenly, she ceases even to be polite, for as she goes up the steps of the auditorium on her way out she turns her head right and left, looks at the seated spectators and tells them in the most offensive terms how much she has disliked the play. Of course, it's my play. But it's also her production. She is spoiling her own creation, she is contributing to her own ruin.

She comes up to me and abuses the play to me, its author. Not even politely. Just offensive nonsense. She has lost her intelligence, she has also lost her good manners. She has definitely tipped over. How will the uncle manage to arrange things? How will he be able to reclaim the lady's threatened portion: a piece of ground with houses that are about to tumble down? Will the barbed wire hold?

The philosopher thinks by philosophizing. The painter thinks by painting; painting is the form of his thought, it is his thought. Architecture and the sciences constitute other specialized forms of thought.

This simply proves that reality, or the world, appears under a multiplicity of aspects to the many and various temperaments of men, who thus experience the world each in his own way and restore it, recreate it, reconstruct it according to the means proper to each of their different vocations, each of them expressing himself differently and, by expressing himself (for creation is expression and vice versa) giving such or such a form, concrete or abstract, philosophical or literary or mathematical, or architectural, or musical, to reality. This is why there are different systems of expression, this is why there is a multiple variety of languages.

When the philosopher philosophizes, when the painter paints, the one is philosophizing about philosophy, the other questioning himself about painting. To philosophize or to paint involves asking questions about these forms of thought.

In my view, a playwright is a man who thinks by writing his dramas or comedies just as the philosopher thinks by philosophizing. At the same time, a dramatic work is a sort of reflection about drama in general. The dialogue and movement of the stage are the author's particular way of exploring reality, of exploring himself, of understanding things and of understanding himself.

The language of literature, particularly of dramatic literature, is by no means an illustration or a vulgarization of some other, superior, language. A concrete thought, a thought by means of images, of happenings, of movements, is as valid, that's to say it is just as proper an instrument of research, as conceptual and discursive language. I mean that it is often supposed that in order to write a play one has, or ought to have,'an idea, or certain ideas, or a coherent set of ideas that must be translated into scenic images, which will illustrate these ideas or doctrines so as to make them more easily understood by the public.

In actual fact, the language of artistic creation is often that which is the most complex, the most charged with meaning; far from having to be determined by some system of thought which is extrinsic or superior to it, and to which it merely has to submit, it's often the artist's language which stimulates and engenders the thought of others, which creates new ways of seeing the world, hence a new mentality. Ideologies, sociologies, systems of aesthetics are nurtured on works of art. There can be no philosophy of culture without culture itself, no philosophical theory without those living examples of psychology, works of art, whose authors did not need to know or take into account the closed experiences of the past. Otherwise there would never have been anything new. This new element, which is knowledge of something, is also construction, of course, since any knowledge, any encounter between the self and the world is a projection of the self into that substance which is the world, a projection, that's to say a pattern, a shape, an architecture.

To sum it all up, let's say that the artist may perhaps not have any ideas at the back of his head, or over the top of his head, which he feels bound to demonstrate. But he has ideas *in his head* which are potentialities, living seeds which shoot up and blossom in their own way, according to their own nature, according to the modalities proper to creation which is a concrete, autonomous form of thought, exploring the world and at the same time constructing it, since all knowledge is projection.

A whole world is built up, or disclosed, as the artist writes it and thinks it.

Practice makes perfect, or, as Raymond Queneau has neatly and wittily put it: *'C'est en forgeant qu'on devient forgeron, c'est en écrivant qu'on devient écriveron.'*

I often find it quite impossible to hold an opinion about a fact, a thing or a person. Since it's all a matter of interpretation, one has to choose a particular interpretation, or rather, one wills it to be valid; it's my will to define things in one particular way and no other, which makes a certain person or a certain thing or a certain event appear thus to me; I wish to give it this interpretation because it suits my interest, my desires, my conscience. I know that my judgment is subjective, not disinterested; so I feel as if all judgment were falling apart, all interpretations disintegrating. I am right, *if I want to be*; that's not enough to entitle me to have an opinion, to be in the right. I'm too scrupulous; not selfish enough to impose my point of view. I can only pass an objective, a 'just' judgment, on myself.

'Reality' is for me only something that I impose on what is, on that which exists, that sort of substance outside myself, or in which I am immersed; I myself am, at the same time, fashioned by that which surrounds me and from which, of course, I have issued, as present-day philosophy tells us only too clearly.

Undoubtedly then the interpretation which I give of this or that is a projection of myself. More particularly, any interpretation that I may give of a thing, a fact, an event is the expression of my group's interest, then of my personal interest, my passion. Of course I interpret it in my own interest (I make it significative as the modern phrase is) according to my wishes, and I ascribe to this event, this being, this person my own intentions or those that suit me: so that to paint anyone's portrait is in fact unconsciously to paint one's own portrait. One gives a meaning to things according to one's own potentialities, according to the power of one's observation or imagination, but these potentialities are also someone's interests.

How is one to be objective? Just? Accurate? How is one to tell the truth? How can one make sure that this is the 'real' truth, not a truth chosen and laid down by me? Is this an unreasonable demand, does it make utter nonsense from a philosophical point of view?

Knowing this (my own way of interpreting things, not the absolute truth) I am undecided, conscious of everybody's subjectivity and of my own, aware that any judgment is relative, true and yet false, impossible, etc. I can only refuse to pass judgment, to give such or such an interpretation of a certain person, of what he or she does, and does to me. I cannot lay down the truth when the truth is only what I want it to be, the projection of my own self-interest, of my selfishness, of my own aggressiveness (not the other person's), of my will to live, of my vitality, of my passion: of my subjectivity. The other person's subjectivity, passion and desire are as valid as mine. (The pure sciences, physics, mathematics, are subjective only in so far as they reflect the structure of our own minds, for of course the physical or mathematical apprehension of pure reality is governed by the resources and configuration of the human mind; they are, however, relatively 'absolute' and objective, in so far as they exclude any direct interest, vulgar passions, emotional, political or sociological interpretations, etc.; thus, corresponding to non-affective mental structures, they are a unique, indisputable and universal field for understanding. This is well known, of course; I am only considering it from the point of view of our psychology.)

I am sure (this is an objective truth) both of my own subjectivity (and that of others) and of the fact that the latter is determined by something 'outside', which is also subjectively acquired, an 'outside' which, being subjectively acquired, is an inside. From this subject–object tangle we can only extricate ourselves by means of some sort of Neo-Platonism (ideas=pure essences: = truly objective truths); I am ready to believe in this, although with mistrust because my wishes are involved; once again, my own subjectivity.

Reason, to the strong, seems foolishness. Reason without strength is madness.

The New Novel

The novelists of this school imagine or describe things for me. I am their prisoner, as at the cinema (the theatre, on the other hand, allows me a certain imaginative freedom).

The description of objects, then, deprives me of all freedom. I have nothing left to do because I have nothing to imagine, the writer makes me a prisoner of things, of objects, he tries to shut me up in a queer fictitious universe, an obsessional world of the imagination.

When I read: here is a door, I can clearly see the door. When I am told: a hand turns the key in the lock to open it, I can clearly see a hand, a key, a lock, a key turning. To say more is superfluous. And it even prevents one from seeing. You're too close to it: you lose all sense of perspective; in this case, the imagination left free would have provided the perspective.

I had come from far away. I had travelled through gloomy towns. I had to tell the truth (which truth? and to whom?); I could find nothing but worn-out parables.

I come back, I see her, I see her again at the end of the voyage I have just made, as mariner (presumably to pay my way) on a boat sailing down a muddy, blackish river; the deck of the boat is grimy too, they wash it with dirty water . . . I find her again (was she expecting me? did she know I was coming back?) when I land at the port of Kishinev. . . .

'I've got some money,' I say, 'let's go for a walk through the town. I've got some money, some bank notes, we'll get back our jobs.' But she is weeping and I cannot comfort her. She has grown old. I embrace her, she's standing naked in a crowd of people, her skin is brownish, she's wearing a pearl necklace round her neck. I clasp her tenderly in my arms, I hug her tight, despairingly: 'I love you,' I tell her, 'we'll both become teachers again. . . . Wipe your tears away, don't swallow your pearls, I implore you.'

From time to time, very rarely, I wake up in my dreams, in a life where I spend most of the time sleeping. I wake up in my dream and recognize her.

The great, auspicious symbols that arise from the depths of the psyche are in my case reversed; they are sinister and baleful. Is my unconscious a peculiar one?

Thus, normally, the father-figure is an auspicious, benevolent one, the father is a guide; for me the father is a monster, a tyrant.

Thus Schäffer, or the baker, or the ballet-master are all father-figures, but they are tyrants. For other people, fire represents light, purification, life, brightness, the sun, but for me it is a symbol and indeed a premonition of death; I dreamed that my mother was in the midst of flames from which I could not rescue her. She had a stroke; she died the next day. I dreamed that my old uncle went into a burning house: he fell ill and died three months later.

For me, earth is not a foster-mother, it means mud, it means decomposition, it means death, which terrifies me. Cellars, the interiors of houses mean shelter for other people; for me, they are tombs. When I dream of the inside of a house, it is always sinking down into the damp earth. Earth does not mean safety to me but decay, something to be struggled against.

Water for me does not mean abundance, nor calm, nor purity. It generally appears to me as dirty, as an image of anguish. Water engulfs one, or at any rate soils one (to soil is to threaten with death). It, too, means decomposition.

Most people, when they try to tell their dreams, interpret them, explain them, talk about them, intervene in them.

A dream is a story or a situation which must be told in the barest way, or just described. Really, one should not relate one's dreams, one should try to give a description of them, for a dream consists not of speech but of images.

Three dreams about the same figure. Three dreams about Schäffer.

I

I pushed open the main gate. I was still wearing my fawn summer cap, under my left arm I had a loaf of bread; the woman journalist was holding my other arm. We went forward about ten yards under the dark archway, then we found ourselves in the inner courtyard of the building, which was almost as dark: on all four sides, six storeys with tall open windows, at the balconies of which the tenants were leaning over to watch the children taking exercise, or having physical training, under the direction of a man of about forty-five or six. He was standing at one of the windows, on the fifth floor, opposite me and a little to the left. Close to the ground, about half way up the ground floor windows, was the net into which children, some quite small, the others nearing adolescence, had to jump from the windows, under the indifferent, helpless or approving gaze of all these grown-ups, some of whom must certainly have been related to them. Jumping into the net was not the most difficult part. Within the net there were tiers of seats. The children had to jump so as to land sitting on these seats in three rows, one above the other.

At one of the windows in the topmost floor, on the opposite side to where the instructor was standing at his window, we saw a girl of thirteen or fourteen who was silently but stubbornly refusing to jump into the net. The instructor beckoned her towards him, and the child's body stretched out, as long and thin as an eel, to where he stood; he put out his arm, took the girl by

135

the hair, and when her face was quite close to his gave her a long kiss on the lips, then sent the poor child tumbling into the net, where she landed duly seated on one of the benches in the third row. Other children jumped from several windows, on the orders of the master, without being pushed, performing the feat success-fully, until at one point the two smallest, who must have been between three and five years old, fell down face forward in the middle of the net, missing the rows of benches. The master grew angry, scolded the children, announced that he was going to come down and punish them; I protested loudly, pointing out that it was almost impossible to land on the front row of seats because they were already occupied by bigger children. How could chil-dren be expected to jump from the top floor and land immediately below the others? I added that the exercises these children were being made to perform were cruel, unreasonable and pointless.

The woman journalist was the only person who agreed with me, or at least who did so publicly, before all these people. But Lolotte, who was an emancipated woman, had the courage of her convictions.

The instructor did in fact come down, and emerged from the dark corridor on my right, where I could see the first steps of the stair that led to the upper floors. I went up to him; he was dressed with taste and elegance, in a smart, well cut navy blue suit; he was bare-headed, and his carefully combed black hair glistened slightly, presumably with brilliantine. He was somewhat above average height, about five foot nine or ten, and well proportioned; he gave an impression of frightening power and great self-assurance. I went up the two steps of the little perron to speak to him, but he meanwhile was walking towards me without hesitation, without any appearance of guilt, quite the reverse, brazen and scornful. He paused at the foot of the stair that led into the courtyard, with one hand on the banister. Being close to him, face to face, I could see that on each of his cheeks there was a great scorch mark, the colour of whisky. Although he was in the wrong, he behaved as though I were. 'You're a cruel bully,' I told him. 'I'm an educator,' he replied. 'Master-at-arms and schoolmaster; I teach these children in my own way. Education is always hard.'

The parents at the windows displayed no reaction, they

136

watched us and listened to us without taking sides, without uttering a word; their impassivity surprised me very much.

'This is not education, it's torture. The lady here agrees with me,' I said, pointing to Lolotte.

'He's quite right,' said the baker, wearing a decoration, who suddenly appeared at my side with his daughter. 'He's right', pointing to the instructor, 'children must get used to Spartan discipline and they must be taught acrobatics.'

'Fascist,' I said to the baker, then turning to the instructor: 'You haven't even a teacher's diploma. You're taking advantage of these people's innocence. My friend here is a journalist and so am I, and we're going to write about all this in the papers. Besides, I'm going right away to ring up the authorities.'

The instructor looked at me with a sneer.

'You can't do anything against me, I know everybody, I shall get any paper banned that dares to meddle with what doesn't concern it, and I shall get the editors sacked. And I shall crush you. You don't know who I am. My name is Schäffer.'

'We shall see,' I said, 'we shall see.' And I backed away from him.

II

I happened to meet Schäffer once again; I had some difficulty in recognizing him. He had lost some of his self-assurance. He had, after all, got into trouble with the police. Not on my account, at least I don't think so, I've forgotten, but I don't think I dared lodge a complaint against him.

It was on the Place de l'Opéra of some great city that I saw him. A black beard hid the scorch marks on his face. Probably he did not want to be recognized. He was a ballet master, and he put on performances that made his country famous throughout the whole world. He went everywhere throughout the world, which did not prevent him from being condemned to penal servitude for life. That is why every time he puts on a show the theatre or the opera-house in which he and his troupe are performing is surrounded with barbed wire, policemen and soldiers with machine guns. When the season is over they handcuff Schäffer again and take him off to gaol until the day when another performance is to be held in some great international capital. Then the officials let him out, under surveillance, to rehearse his company, and send him, well guarded, to the foreign country in question, whose police undertake not to let him escape.

'Why have you been condemned?' I asked him, in the great empty square with a cordon of police all round us.

'Because they discovered,' said Schäffer, leaning on his stick (had he hurt his leg? had he a slight limp?) 'that when I was a child I killed my little brother with a knife.'

'A child is not responsible.'

'Of course it wouldn't be important if I had just stabbed him with a knife. But what was considered very serious and quite unpardonable was that I cut him in two, I sawed him across the middle; so I'm in prison for life, because they're afraid I might do it again. A funny situation, being famous and infamous both at once; I travel throughout the world, and strange though it may seem, I am a prisoner; posses of police, chains and handcuffs go with me everywhere to theatres, opera houses, grand hotels. I have great powers, since I direct all these ballerinas,' he said, showing me hundreds of young girls behind the row of policemen, all running towards the steps of the Opera House, 'I have power and at the same time I am powerless.'

III

The third time I saw Schäffer he had sunk even lower. He seemed to be hiding, to have been forced to cheat, he was an outcast.

I was standing in front of a great blank wall with a door in it. What was the door for? Beyond the wall there was nothing except the same muddy earth as on this side, under a dark lowering sky. Where had I come from? I didn't know. From a long way off, surely, to have landed here in front of this wall. My legs were muddied to the knee, it was raining, and I was shivering, having neither coat nor hat. There were no trees under which I could shelter, I'd been crazy to leave home. I suddenly remembered Lolotte. When I find a telephone box I'll ring her. I thought, she'll come and fetch me in her car. But where could I find a telephone box, in weather like this? I leaned against the wall to keep my back dry, at least. Where was I? Was I a tourist? What was this dark muddy country? And that was when, remembering that I had got out of a train, I also remembered Schäffer and the splendour and shame of his travels. It was just as if I had summoned him. Suddenly the muddy, empty square was filled with proletarians and militiamen, at any rate with people who seemed to be proletarians and others who seemed to be militiamen, to judge by the ferocity or malevolence with which they were glaring.

Dressed in a long black cassock, a big round, broad-brimmed hat, a great black beard, a shabby kind of rabbi or schoolmaster was marching towards me, singing as he went, followed by a whole class of small Jewish children, also wearing black cassocks, hats, long black beards and curl-papers.

I immediately recognized Schäffer. What a curious man; however wretched, however much of an outcast he might be he was still determined to lord it over other wretches.

'Schäffer,' I called out to him.

He did not answer. He went on walking, singing and intoning with his schoolboys. He passed quite close to me. I took advantage of this to grab him by the sleeve.

'Hush,' he said, 'hush.'

'I recognized you,' I whispered. 'This is an atheistic, Marxist country, how do they allow you and your children to chant these prayers?'

'I've found a way out. Instead of singing verses of the Bible and the Psalms of David, the children sing and recite the Communist Party Manifesto.'

'But that's against your principles. You're teaching them to be anti-religious.'

'No,' replied Schäffer, 'for these children recite and sing the Manifesto in Hebrew. They have learnt it by heart, but they don't understand Hebrew. Religion is not in danger; in this way everything's safe, or at any rate I get away with it. Hush,' he repeated, going off in the rain with his black-clad, bearded little children.

The decadence of Schäffer, proud Schäffer, although I disliked him, saddened me so much that my mouth was filled with black hairpins and I began to spit them out as I walked away, but the more I spat out the more there were, and as I went I scattered them all over the road and it became quite black, covered with black hairpins.

In my controversies, in my conflicts, I am always handicapped and in a way disarmed from the start, for the fact of knowing that I am neither right nor wrong gives me an uneasy conscience. Yet, since I have after all some vocation for objectivity, I realize at the same time the reality of my subjectivity and also the profound subjectivity of other people. This subjectivity distorts reality, makes it impossible to know. And yet this is such an elementary sort of subjectivity, of which people could so easily become aware, since it is based on prejudice, on petty individual interests, on unsatisfied wishes, on personal claims which the claimants pretend are disinterested and objective, and set forward as a moral right. I know what mean and unworthy feelings, what lust for power and greed for gain most people conceal when they adopt an attitude, when they 'choose' a party. Behind so much ideology there lurk private passions which make for insincerity, which corrupt and invalidate the worth of an attitude whose apparent generosity must not deceive us. . . . Or else, we must admit that all desires are justified.

But that's what the real lie consists of, that's the crime: lying to oneself, being in disharmony with one's own truth, one's own innermost knowledge of things, as revealed through one's consciousness. Objectivity, in fact, means just this: to be in harmony with one's own subjectivity, not to lie to oneself.

This fact, this reality, has no other meaning than that which I give it, which I choose or am able to give it. . . .
But I should like to give no further meaning to anything. To do away with meanings. . . . I don't like tyrannizing, I don't like being tyrannized over.
Tyranny is like Proteus; under its manifold masks there is always Proteus.

History is cunning, a famous statesman said. People are so

credulous, History takes them all in. Things always happen differently. It's never what you thought.

Ideas are never realized in History; History impairs our ideas, in fact it runs counter to ideas; the fact is that we wanted something different from what we thought we wanted. Our ideas were merely the impulses of our various emotional masks, and these attain reality by impairing those ideas which were only substitutes for the impulses.

I am told, in a dream: 'You can only find the key to the riddles, you can only get the answer to all your questions through a dream. You must dream that dream.' So, in my dream, I fall asleep, and I dream, in my dream, that I'm having that absolute, revealing dream. I wake up, in my dream. I remember, in my dream, the dream of a dream, and now 'I know', and an immense, serene joy possesses me. When I wake up, really wake up, I clearly re-member having dreamed that I dreamed, I remember having dreamed that I dreamed the revealing dream, but I remember nothing at all about its content, and once again the dream that explains everything, that dream of absolute truth, has eluded me.

It was a complicated scene: the slope of a hill, little gardens, a great deal of damp dark earth, grey autumn skies. What else was there? A white cat coming out of the kitchen garden, a bare garden without plants, in which everything was newly sown (or had been gathered already, which is not the same thing at all). I discover that the cat has turned into a young lady. We are sitting at a long rustic table inside some farm, and the girl, dressed in white, says: 'I'm tired of my fiancé. I've got to get away from his authority, from my family, I need my freedom, I must develop my own personality.' Presumably this was why the white cat had escaped through the open wicket-gate of the enclosure. She was running and I was trying to catch her. 'It's the same with me,' I told her at table. 'I'm wondering and trying to decide what to do.' Then scraps of images, a peasant with a moustache, wearing a cap. Suddenly the peasant is myself, instead of my interlocutor; apples—did they fall from that apple-tree? (is it an apple-tree?)— around which people are talking to me about money, the crowd of people round the apple-tree, all of us in a little enclosed meadow, an orchard, but why no spring sunshine, why this dark lowering sky?

The peasant was counting his pence, I watched him; then I became like him once more, a peasant with a cap and a moustache, as if I were his reflection or he were my reflection in a mirror. I know who that peasant is it's Schäffer again (and where's the key, the dream of dreams that will reveal the truth?).

He feels no more surprise. He is accustomed now to seeing walls rise up in front of him, but instead of passing round them he per-sists in trying to knock them down with his fists. Then he gives up, and moves away. He upsets inkpots, making the tablecloths all black and sticky; in vain he tries to mop up the ink; he dirties clean cloths, he blackens his hands, his arms, his clothes. The more he tries to clean things up the dirtier he makes them, makes everything. Look, even his face is covered with ink.

'He's blackened the pages of his new notebook too, you can't see what he'd written. The floor is all black and sticky and so are the walls.'

'He writes too much, he doesn't like what he writes. He ought just to rub it out. No, he covers it up, he hides it but he keeps it.'

'Like a cat burying its excrement.'

What right have you to pretend that your dreams are em-bodied, your images materialized in other people, what right have you to invent characters and worlds?

Are such inventions 'true'? They are so true that there's an endless production of literature, poetry, painting and plays all over the earth. People are for ever talking about imaginary characters, they produce a little literature and still more literature about literature, and literature about literary literature. Works of psychology, psychoanalysis, sociology, metaphysics, aesthetics of course and the philosophy of culture, are almost all based on the productions of the imagination.

I dream that I have only one molar left in my top jaw and that it has grown loose; in fact I pick it out with my fingers; the tooth is long, with a deep root. I put it back, I push it in with my fingers, but it will hardly stay in place.

Our friend has just died. Here is his empty study, with his books, his photograph. Out of all the people we have known the dead are already far more numerous than the living. When shall we learn to hope for death instead of dreading it? We should attain the state of mind of the Mexicans of old, for whom death was an occasion for rejoicing. The whole of humanity should be reorganized in this direction; civilization has got off to a bad start by staking everything on existence, on life, on history and on politics. It's because we have staked everything on life that we are incapable of living.

I dreamed of a voyage. Several hours have passed since I awoke, and almost all the images have disappeared into the abyss of daylight, that other sort of night. The deck of an enormous dark boat. Will they give us a good cabin? I don't want, on any account to sleep in a communal dormitory. But we are not on the boat deck after all, only on the main platform of the harbour station, which is roofed in, that's why it is so dark. We can't make this voyage, for one of our three suitcases has disappeared. I had not put my name on the case, nor my initials, and yet things are usually so well organized that cases don't get lost. Besides, all these other travellers are carrying cases without names on them. And yet are these really station platforms? Or are we really on the enormous deck of the boat? If that is so, where's the case with my suits in it? Fortunately the case with my manuscript in it is there, that's what matters, she tells me, that's where our real wealth lies. Wasn't there something else in the lost case, weren't there manuscripts and notebooks as well? Your suitcase must be at Lyons, a traveller tells me, and in any case if you want to go on that cruise to the East you must leave from Paris. 'In Paris,' I say, 'there are airports of course, but there's no harbour station, perhaps one would have to take the plane for a harbour station somewhere else. I don't like flying, I'm afraid of flying, and yet I'll take the plane if I have to, I mustn't be more of a coward than all these young men in uniform.' Then I wonder if it's really an airport that they have in Paris; is there or isn't there a harbour station? I try to remember but I cannot.

This dream forms part of a certain cycle of dreams. I have already sailed on the same boat, which is broader than it is long; so broad that in one of my later dream voyages it almost touched both sides of the Bosphorus. Journeys on this boat are usually very pleasant, but none the less disturbing, vaguely disturbing, as though the pleasantness were only an illusion, something concealing a trap.

On either side of the Bosphorus we could see houses that were dark green or a red so dark as to be almost black, then suddenly a sort of lock which, somebody told us, was the frontier, the end of the Bosphorus. I was now standing not on the deck of the boat but on one of the banks. From here I could see the other bank, in the light of a setting sun that set the whole horizon ablaze. On the deck of the huge boat, another time, we found the way down to the ballroom, which was full of people, women in lace dresses, white against the darkness, lace caps, brides of all ages.

That time I had not seen the sea; last night I did not catch a glimpse of it either, for it was hidden by the prow of the boat, or the end of the platform or the inside of the station. And during the voyage to Constantinople, it was not the sea that I saw but rather a river, almost entirely hidden by the boat, with a little green water on the right, a little green water on the left, and then the lock, with white foam. Have I ever dreamed of the sea?

How right that man in the street was—probably a philosopher —who said to me: 'How much easier and nicer everything would be if it weren't for sickness and death and if people got on together!'

'And if the sun shone all the time and it was never too hot or too cold.'

'Oh . . . that would perhaps be asking too much!'

We have just been rehearsing *Thirst and Hunger*. The first stage, when one is terrified of being betrayed, is over. When one sees one's characters taking concrete shape, when one sees one's nightmares being materialized, one no longer recognizes them, one's afraid of recognizing them, one refuses to recognize them.

Nowadays criticism seems increasingly to have one sole aim to repudiate and destroy a work. If you reduce a work to its psychological content, it becomes merely the stuff of psychology; reduced to its social context it is merely the stuff of sociology. Or else people try to reduce a work to the general ideas which it contains and illustrates; or else they try to make it the instrument of some political or ideological system, such as Marxism or another. . . .

In reality, a work of art is irreducible. It *is* just what remains after, or in spite of, sociology, psychoanalysis, economics, ideologico-political systems, philosophy and so forth.

Thus instead of illuminating a work, criticism leaves it in darkness and sheds light only on its context. The important thing is not with what a work can be identified; what's important, what's essential, is the fact of being something different, since it's in so far as it stands apart from its context that it is of value.

The misguided critics of today merely echo Taine's mistake. But the authority to whom they refer is no longer Taine but Marx, who at a pinch can be considered a slightly inferior Taine. The work is the product of a *milieu*, an epoch, a race, said Taine, as everybody knows. The work is the product of a class, a society, a time, say the Marxists, those neo-Tainists most, indeed all, works of art are the products of their time (and of many other things, and of something outside time, but that's another question), of course, but how does it happen that works of art are different from one another? That's the objection that was made to Taine, and that can be made to contemporary critics, the Tainists of today. To study contexts and conditionings is interesting, of course; but the context is one thing, the work of art is another. They try to swamp the work, they try to dissolve it in its context, they try to destroy it. One would like to protest 'Murderers!' except that one knows that a work of art is indestructible. After a certain lapse of time, contexts cease to be important, they broaden out, but the monuments of art remain indissolubly themselves and include their 'contexts', redeeming these from oblivion.

Love: to love means letting oneself be loved, consenting to belong to someone, it means more or less renouncing oneself, allowing someone else to have control over one, not out of a liking for submission nor out of masochism, but in order not to dispossess the other person, for whom this would mean suffering and, more or less, death. Valéry's definition of love loving means making use of someone to satisfy an imagined need . . . is at the opposite pole from mine.

It is a mistaken, or rather a typically Western, point of view. It's because they think in this way (for this definition of love is the exact opposite of love, since true love means giving and not possession) that the French, for instance, do not love, won't submit, want freedom or else possession; there is utter confusion between having and being. The fact is that they have reached the point of not loving themselves, of not loving others, of detesting themselves in others and others in themselves; the French do not love, since they know only a sense of possession.

This explains fairly obviously their hatred of 'others', for they are afraid of becoming those others' tools. Herein lies the narrow-mindedness, the egotism which is displayed in French policy. This policy can be summed up in a sentence or two: I don't mind hurting or annoying so-and-so, provided I can annoy somebody else. Spouting justice and charity they practise a shocking, petty-bourgeois, Leftist meanness. The Right wing had the courage of its hates, did not profess any absolute moral claims.

Jean D. was telling me about a certain great contemporary writer who couldn't have been much older than myself. We were at a friend's house and there was a big party going on.

I had been drinking a little, Jean D. had been drinking more than I, everybody had been drinking. It was happening amidst the hubbub and the smoke and the fumes of alcohol. When one tries to recall such evenings, one's mental pictures are confused: a world with blurred contours, gaps in one's memory, black holes, as in recollections of dreams.

'You know,' Jean said to me, 'he's in a bad way. He's gone white, his legs are unsteady, his hands shake, he's done for.'

I know some people, some intellectuals who preserve their

clarity of mind and their vitality much longer. What's the use? More or less all one had to do, more or less all one could do, has been done. You have to play the game: one, two, three and off you go. The sense of futility paralyses me again; not quite, for I fight against it; so long as each day seems to me a miracle, so long as I'm able to love, able to think, able to remember, able to write. . . . So long as I don't repeat myself. . . . I know, though, that I'm nearing the end of the holidays. The day after tomorrow I shall be an old man, a healthy one maybe but there's nothing more odious than a young old man. I can't see myself becoming a wise old man. There's still today, there's still tomorrow, then I shall really have to retire into the wings. I settle down in the moment, I surround myself with the walls of the moment, I shelter under the roof of the moment. In short, to have thirty years ahead of one, or twenty, or two years, or two days, means the same thing for the moment. But I don't want decay to take me unawares, to seize hold of me treacherously, to clasp me in its rotting arms, which infect what they hold with rottenness. They'll have to let me know, to give me warning before I go blind and deaf.

It's not possible that there should be no beginning again. So many parts to be played! I shall become a seed once more, I shall be reborn. I shall have to start earlier. I shall have to love more, to love better, I shall have to breathe more deeply, more freely.

I look at things. I calm down. I am just as I was yesterday and the day before. Unfortunately, if I look ahead I see the precipice getting closer and closer, and the rocks on which my head will be shattered when I tumble down and go on rolling without being able to stop.

How did it all begin for me? The roots of memories must surely lie deep in what has been forgotten in a chaos of darkness, swarming with unknown urges, desires, impulses, anxieties which I shall never be able to disclose but which I feel, which direct me, which are stirring within me and impel me to act. If I knew the original reasons for all my actions I should cease to act. There is no reason for reasons. There is no reason for anything. If I knew, if I could see, could understand, I should return to silence and night. I think that if what impels me to live could be explained to me I should stop living.

147

For the time being, or ever since the beginning, if I go on living it's because my will not to exist is kept down, dominated by my thirst for existence. These two wills are in permanent conflict, and it's this conflict which is the drama, the anguish that fills my life with disquiet, with a sense of guilt and of remorse. The happy man is the one who loves living, without any mental reservation, who is not obsessed by the idea of death and for whom death, since it is not an obsession, holds no terrors. Am I to die without having known myself, without having understood myself?

Is the individual self, the personality an essential reality? or is the self an illusion? That's to say: is the personality to be taken into account? And is it to be taken into account as much as, or less or more than, the group? Is the group, on the other hand, to be considered as 'truer', as having a less illusory reality than the individual?

If the individual self is an illusion, it seems clear to me that the group is also an illusion; in that case everything is illusion, which is quite possible. And yet the illusion itself can have a certain truth or reality (since it can be defined or named) which must be taken into account, whether it be an illusion of self, of nation, of race, of other groups, of the world.

I do not exist, in so far as I am not free: in so far as I am conditioned, determined, solely by external forces, urges, dynamisms of which I am merely the battlefield, the meeting-place, one of countless meeting-places (but I am at least this particular meeting-place). But since the group too is determined by impulses (social, biological, physical, cosmic) we have merely transferred elsewhere the problem of our search for non-illusory reality: for groups, too, are meeting-places for conflicting forces.

The 'I' is the fruit of a situation which is determined, created by its setting; the 'we' is merely another 'I'; it is the fruit of a more extensive conditioning; groups, too, are determined by their setting. Thus I am no more illusory than the group is. The individual self has, moreover, the advantage of being the most powerful and tenacious of illusions. Besides, as I have said, the illusion has in any case its own sort of truth.

Aggression against the individual self, the denial of the personality, seems to me to be, consciously or not, the belated fruit of the two main collectivist trends of our century: Nazism and Left-wing totalitarianism (as realized in history). (The personalist philosophy of Emmanuel Mounier and his journal *Esprit* had overcome this problem at one time, and provided an answer; how urgently we now feel the need for a new personalism!) If the individual self is an illusion, who's to prevent me from repudiating it, from destroying and despising it, from killing or imprisoning my fellow men?

And yet the fact that there is such a relentless attack on the personality suggests that basically it is still believed in, that it is not considered an illusion, that people believe in it so strongly that they want to destroy it. Other selves are resented as rivals by those who deny the self. Yesterday's politicians, today's ideologists, all those who deny individualism are fierce and violent individualists, impelled by a pathological will to power and an excessive urge to assert themselves, to realize themselves, to absorb or dominate others so that only their own hypertrophied self may survive: personalities, races, works, signatures, everything must be submerged in the collective impersonalism, in the collective unconscious, except that self which denounces the presence of the *others* whom he seeks to drive out from his own being.

I am this particular eddy. In this broad river there are innumerable eddies. In each eddy the same water is whirling round as in all the rest of the river: foul, or clear, or muddy, or bearing leaves, plants, bits of branches. When the waters sink, the eddies seem to disappear. But they are still there, virtually. The waters rise again: the eddies reappear.

The water, which is the same in all the eddies in the stream, is as it were the substance of the eddy. But the dynamic form of this eddy, its structure, its movement are different from all the rest: one is more rapid, another less dangerous, another has a broad swirling motion, a different architecture in movement, a different rhythm.

Every eddy is an individual self. Its organization, its particular movement are its personality. The self is a particular organization. Every eddy is different from all the others. Nobody is another person. Every eddy is anarchical. Every eddy has its own reality, which is evident and not illusory, according to the way it organizes the river water which is common to all. Every self both affirms and denies the group. Every self is both social and anti-social. Thus it exists, it asserts itself. Everything is a sign.

You never bathe twice in the same river. Maybe. The waters flow, and there are other waters. But each of us makes up his own eddy, which is always the same.

The eddies will disappear perhaps. But not until the universal river disappears.

I am so very true that I cannot escape from myself. I organize myself. I am the self that organizes myself thus, arranging the same materials in a unique pattern.